IMAGES
of America

ORGANIZED CRIME
IN MIAMI

Joseph Fischetti, brother of notorious Chicago mobsters Charlie and Rocco Fischetti, confidently poses while waterskiing in Miami Beach. Operating from the Magic City, Joe maintained substantial connections to major crime figures around the country, as well as a close friendship with Frank Sinatra, which the gangster parlayed into lucrative business deals throughout South Florida. Read all about the Fischetti family and their Miami exploits in the opening pages of chapter five, "Swimming with the Fishes." (Author's collection.)

ON THE COVER: Arrested with three companions, Al Capone (center) hides his face as he and his cohorts are led to a downtown Miami police station. In May 1930, Miami police continually harassed Capone, with multiple arrests for investigation or vagrancy. Capone's lawyers sued the city for harassment and false imprisonment; however, Capone would be charged with two counts of perjury for statements made in his harassment claims. After a three-day trial, Judge E.C. Collins acquitted Capone of the perjury charges. (HistoryMiami Museum, 1989-011-19510.)

IMAGES
of America

ORGANIZED CRIME
IN MIAMI

Avi Bash

ARCADIA
PUBLISHING

Published by Arcadia Publishing
Charleston, South Carolina

Library of Congress Control Number: 2016935373

For all general information, please contact Arcadia Publishing:
Telephone 843-853-2070
Fax 843-853-0044
E-mail sales@arcadiapublishing.com
For customer service and orders:
Toll-Free 1-888-313-2665

Visit us on the Internet at www.arcadiapublishing.com

*The author would like to dedicate this book to his father,
Yossi, and the loving memory of his mother, Vicki.*

CONTENTS

ACKNOWLEDGMENTS

I would like to express my gratitude to those who have assisted throughout the process of this book, whether through contributions, support, insight, or feedback. This completed work would not have been possible without the following: Dawn Hugh, Kristen Kotowski, and Ashley Trujillo of the HistoryMiami Research Center; Gordon Winslow, Patty Pauzuolis, and Allison Hooper of the Miami-Dade Municipal Archives; the State Archives of Florida; Caitrin Cunningham and Katelyn Carter of Arcadia Publishing; John Binder; Marnix Brendel; Geoff Schumacher and the Mob Museum staff; Casey Piket; Scott Deitche; the estate of Thomas McGinty; the Estate of Nicholas Fischetti; Viki Varon Armstrong; Jim from Boston; Yossi and Whiskey Bash; Stacy, Travis, Layla, and Liam Gibb; Aaron and Pnina Sobel; David J. Berkowitz; Bryan Rubin; Jesse Stamler; and most important, the law enforcement, public officials, newspapermen, and photographers who tirelessly combated and exposed organized crime. Without their meticulously documented findings and reporting, none of this research would have been possible.

INTRODUCTION

At the time of the great Florida land boom of the 1920s, hundreds of thousands of Americans began flooding South Florida looking to start a new life in what developers audaciously referred to as a "tropical paradise." The sudden influx of residents and tourists, along with rapidly developing city amenities, earned Miami its everlasting nickname, the "Magic City." But as with any highly populated metropolitan area, Miami residents and their guests would seek an exciting, vice-filled nightlife to counterpoise the relaxing, calm afternoons lounging on Miami's white-sand beaches. These new Miami locals desired nightclubs, gambling, and most important, liquor, the latter of which happened to be illegal due to the recently ratified 19th amendment that banned the sale and consumption of said product. Mobsters from around the country who were happy to provide these illegal yet highly profitable illicit services found Miami to be the perfect refuge from law enforcement or rival gangs. Individuals from crime families spanning the nation were eager to volunteer their services and set up shop in the quickly budding Miami business market. It was at this time that the American mafia would begin heading south to trade in their suits and fedoras for swim trunks and flip-flops.

Despite the arrival of earlier national crime figures, the county first recognized Miami as a gangsters' paradise when newspaper headlines broadcast the arrival of Chicago mob boss Al Capone and his intentions to plant roots in Miami's rich soil. By the 1930s, Prohibition was a thing of the past, and the Great Depression was ravaging the country's economy. Knowing that financially stable Americans looking for an escape were traveling to South Florida, mobsters arrived in bulk and set up their largest enterprise, one that would provide an everlasting foot in Magic City's door—illegal gambling.

In many aspects, Miami has always been an open city, and the same is true with respect to the mob's arrival and its subsequent impact on the city's development. Representatives from crime syndicates in New York, Chicago, Detroit, Cleveland, and other major metropolises worked harmoniously among each other with little conflict for the first half of the 20th century. These polished criminals understood that dividing territory, splitting operations, and sharing profits would keep internal crime down and, more important, draw little publicity—a necessity for the continual success of their illegal operations. The swift growth of Miami Beach and its surrounding cities was also a welcomed phenomenon to the local law enforcement officers elected and entrusted to patrol the area. When worthless orange groves and mangrove swamps were wondrously transformed into casinos and nightclubs, local sheriffs and deputies ignored orders from state officials and eagerly accepted bribes to ensure that illegal casinos and bookie joints ran smoothly for their new favorite locals.

For more than two decades, gangsters flocking to Miami discovered that the Magic City was, in fact, magical. Besides the perfect year-round climate and enormous profits, Miami also provided convenient access to neighboring countries in which the mob held prosperous business interest. With a short trip by boat, or even shorter by plane, mobsters could easily access Cuba, the Bahamas, and other surrounding Caribbean islands where their gambling establishments were booming. Utilizing profits from their gambling enterprises, crime figures began to invest in real estate and legitimate businesses, further embedding their influence within the community and blurring the line between crook and honest businessmen.

By the mid-1940s, the American mafia had fully infiltrated Miami, with nearly all hotels allowing gambling and open wagering from bookie concessions conveniently located on the premises. Hotels like the Sands, Wofford, and Grand were owned and operated by known mobsters and quickly became local hangouts for visiting gangsters and associates. Seemingly overnight, organized crime figures began buying land, homes, and winter residences in Miami's most prominent neighborhoods, as well as donating to local charities and organizations, greatly contributing to the community's tremendous development. As the 1950s rolled in, little seemed to be able to interrupt the flow of cash generated from the mob's various activities—that is, until Tennessee senator Estes Kefauver launched a campaign to investigate, expose, and eliminate illegal gambling in the United States. With television in its relative infancy, the heavily publicized Kefauver Committee hearings aired to a shocked nation, vividly bringing to life the existence of the mafia and the individuals controlling it. With the assistance of crusading public officials, Kefauver exposed South Floridians to the high level of corruption running rampant throughout their cities. Ritzy casinos were ordered shut, bookmakers whose identities were revealed in the local papers were forced from town, and gangsters from across the country understood that the Magic City had finally lost its magic.

Forced to move their larger gambling operations to Cuba and Las Vegas, organized crime figures who were eager to stay in Miami transitioned their interest into legitimate enterprises. With their vast real estate holdings, they opened hotels, restaurants, and lounges throughout Miami Beach and its surrounding areas. Though these legitimate businesses were established to launder money and serve as a front for illegal enterprises, many became popular nightspots where vacationing tourists could observe laid-back hoodlums and their associates. Law enforcement officers keeping tabs on arriving criminals found it difficult to differentiate between vacation and vice, noting that almost every mob boss in the country wintered in South Florida.

At the start of the 1960s, Miami's landscape and culture continued to evolve, with its most profound transformation resulting in Fidel Castro's overthrowing of the Cuban government. Tens of thousands of Cuban émigrés settled in Miami and quickly adjusted to their new environment, developing what would eventually be referred to as Little Havana, a Cuban-influenced neighborhood noted for its street life, restaurants, and cultural activities. American gangsters, many of whom had spent a great deal of time in pre-Castro Cuba, increased their illegal gambling operations and provided homesick Cubans with a familiar pastime widely played back home—bolita.

Although organized crime was heavily present in Miami, violent crime on the syndicate's behalf was not. While gangland slayings were commonplace in cities like New York and Chicago, the turf wars often stayed on their home soil. Mobsters in Miami understood and respected the rules of operating in an open city, until a 1960s surge in crime led to bombings and murder on the streets of Miami. This new wave of violence perhaps served as a precursor, setting the stage for the all-out drug wars that would terrorize Miami throughout the 1970s and 1980s. By the time of this new radical era, organized crime—in the sense of romanticized figures emphasizing honor, respect, and loyalty—was a thing of the past.

In today's vibrant city of Miami, among the colorful art deco buildings of South Beach and the breathtaking turquoise waters of Biscayne Bay, organized crime is just as prevalent as during the city's formative years—if not more so. In the new millennium, the Italian and Jewish mobs, with their gambling, extortion, and loan-sharking operations, have been eclipsed by Eastern European syndicates committing a variety of high-profile crimes, including credit card fraud, cybercrime, and human trafficking. As the city continues to grow and remains among the country's top tourist destinations, organized criminals—always keeping up with the latest trends and technology—will continue to utilize Miami as a base of operations while siphoning millions of dollars from the city, taxpayers, and businesses.

One

PROHIBITION AND THE FLORIDA LAND BOOM

With the increase of automobile purchases and the completion of Henry Flagler's Florida East Coast Railway, middle-class Americans finally had access to South Florida, making it no longer just a retreat for the elderly, rich, and ill. The land boom of the 1920s—coinciding neatly with another American phenomenon, Prohibition—resulted in the development of a prosperous economy where both honest businessmen and those with a more questionable moral compass could come to make a quick buck. Above, a group of lawmen from Florida's east coast proudly display sacks of confiscated alcohol following a 1920s Prohibition raid. (State Archives of Florida.)

By 1920, the great Florida land boom was in full effect, and investors from across the nation purchased and sold land to cash in on the rapidly appreciating property values. Throughout South Florida, wetlands were drained, and forests were cleared to make room for the seemingly never-ending new development projects. The promotional photograph above, published by the Florida Real Estate Investment Corporation (based in Chicago, Illinois), shows a casino, bathhouse, and boardwalk along central Florida's east coast. Photographs such as this were widely circulated by land speculators looking to attract outside investors. Below is a bird's-eye view of Biscayne Boulevard near Bayfront Park during the height of the land boom. With populations growing at such an abrupt pace, cities found it difficult to keep up with the demand for housing and parking. (Both, State Archives of Florida.)

On January 16, 1920, around the same time Miami's land boom began, the 18th Amendment to the US Constitution took effect, and a nationwide constitutional ban prohibited the sale, production, importation, consumption, and transportation of any alcoholic beverage. Above, women supporters of Prohibition meet at the Casa Loma Hotel in Coral Gables for a tea social in honor of Carry Nation, an early leader of the temperance movement. (State Archives of Florida.)

Once Prohibition took effect, "wet" residents turned to bootleggers and speakeasies to quench their thirst for the illegal beverage. Above, Miami-Dade law enforcement officers show off their spoils following a Prohibition raid in the basement of a South Florida home. Such raids were commonplace, and officers relished posing alongside busted moonshine stills and stacked up boxes of confiscated goods. (State Archives of Florida.)

During Prohibition, seaplanes like the one pictured above offered daily flights to Bimini and Nassau, where tourists and residents could legally drink following a short flight from Miami. Recognizing the money that could be generated, many otherwise honest pilots and captains turned to smuggling and utilized their planes and boats as a vessel for sneaking illegal liquor into Miami from the Caribbean. Rumrunners navigating the waters between the Caribbean islands and South Florida constantly found themselves in a cat-and-mouse game with the US Coast Guard, trying to evade or outrun their ships. Below, an unlucky South Florida rumrunner is captured with 1,500 gallons of booze aboard his ship. (Both, State Archives of Florida.)

At the height of the land boom, Miami Beach became the hottest tourist attraction in the United States. With liquor readily accessible, visitors eager for action were soon greeted by an assortment of nightclubs and casinos along Florida's Gold Coast. Constructed and owned by prominent Miami residents like John Collins and Carl Fisher, bathing casinos like the Roman Pools (above) and the Sunny Isles Casino (below) offered wealthy tourists a variety of activities, including nightly floor shows, bathhouses, beachside picnics, and the lesser-advertised but highly profitable backroom gambling. These early nightclubs and casinos set the stage for the mob-owned casinos that would sweep across the region in the following decade. (Above, author's collection; below, State Archives of Florida.)

By the summer of 1926, Miami's land boom was fizzling and finally concluded following a devastating hurricane that ravaged much of Miami on September 18, 1926. As a result of the destruction, developers were forced into bankruptcy, and the city fell into a financial crisis, signaling an early start to the country's Great Depression. Following the hurricane, major roadways were congested with capsized boats, broken cars, and debris from the abundant open construction sites in the vicinity. Above, a row of boats washed ashore during the 1926 hurricane sits along Bay Shore Drive. Below, an aerial view shows the damage caused to the Roman Pools' bathing casino and the adjacent newly constructed Roney Plaza Hotel. (Both, State Archives of Florida.)

Two

SCARFACE SETTLES SOUTH

Of all the organized crime figures of the 20th century, no name is singularly more recognizable than that of Alphonse Capone. In 1920s Chicago, Capone built a criminal enterprise consisting of bootlegged liquor, gambling, and prostitution that generated an estimated $100 million a year. Needing a break from the empire he built, as well as his rivals and law enforcement pursuing him, Capone set his sights on Florida. After frequent visits to the Sunshine State, he purchased a permanent residence on Palm Island in 1928. (Author's collection.)

Upon his first official visit to the Magic City, Al Capone visited Miami police chief H. Leslie Quigg (left) to state his intentions in South Florida. Before the police force and gathered newspapermen, Capone declared he was in Miami for its healthy climate and a winter vacation with his wife, son, and mother. Quigg warned Capone, "You can stay as long as you behave yourself." (Author's collection.)

Renting out a penthouse suite at the Ponce De Leon Hotel on Flagler Street, Capone befriended Parker Henderson Jr., the eager and impressionable hotel operator who was thrilled with being accepted into Capone's inner circle. Recognizing Henderson's desire to impress, the gang chieftain routinely called on him to run errands, including picking up and endorsing money orders totaling over $30,000 and purchasing a dozen firearms, one of which would later be used in the high-profile 1928 gangland killing of Frankie Yale. (Author's collection.)

Parker Henderson Jr. (right), the portly and gullible manager of the Ponce De Leon Hotel, is photographed with his father, former Miami mayor Parker Henderson Sr. (center), and an unidentified young relative. When word got out that Capone was seeking a winter residence, real estate agents from around Miami began calling Henderson to set a meeting with the big guy. Henderson called his friend Newton Lummus, mayor of Miami Beach, and together, they decided if anyone would be selling property to Capone, it ought to be them. After viewing several places, Capone decided on a two-story white stucco home located on Palm Island. Anticipating the public's reaction to discovering their newest resident was none other than the infamous Al Capone, Lummus suggested that Henderson sign the warranty deed for the property. On March 27, 1928, the transaction closed, and within six months, Henderson officially transferred the deed to Al's wife, Mae Capone. (HistoryMiami Museum, 2010-439-5.)

Capone purchased his palatial estate at 93 Palm Avenue for $40,000 but quickly spent an estimated $100,000 in home improvements and fortifications. Dwelling enhancements included the construction of a solid seven-foot concrete wall surrounding the property, along with iron gates at the entrance, and the replacement of the one-car garage with a two-story lodge house in which the second floor served as a watchtower. Toward the rear of the property, Capone installed the largest boat dock in the vicinity and the largest privately owned swimming pool with a filtration system that handled both seawater and freshwater. Capone spared no expense and paid for the best materials and labor while personally supervising the construction. (Both, author's collection.)

The Capone residence was originally built in 1921 by developer Clarence M. Busch and his partner, Locke T. Highleyman. Both Busch and the home's first owner, insurance broker James W. Popham, were furious when they learned the actual buyer of the home was the notorious Al Capone. Busch, who lived next door to Capone at 94 Palm Avenue, participated in a series of meetings held by the Palm and Hibiscus Islands Improvement Association to find a way to oust Capone. However, the association eventually considered the situation hopeless and dropped it. After two years of neighboring with Capone, Busch wrote to Florida governor Doyle Carlton to voice his complaints, which included violations of building restrictions, loud noise and gunshots, and depreciation of property value as a result of Capone's presence. (Both, author's collection.)

As Capone became acclimated to his new surroundings, he knew it would be necessary to acquire local friends of importance and influence within the community. When Parker Henderson Jr. brought Capone to Sewell Brothers clothing store (above), Capone quickly won over the friendship of Jack Sewell, son of former Miami mayor John Sewell (above left) and nephew of three-time Miami mayor E.G. Sewell (left). On his first visit to the downtown Miami clothing store, Capone spent more than $1,000 purchasing silk shirts, ties, socks, underwear, and other accoutrements. His visit made such an impression that store manager Jack Sewell gifted Capone a $100 panama hat. Much to his family's chagrin, Jack continued his friendship with Capone, which included frequent visits to the Palm Island Villa and even impromptu sparring matches with Capone in his backyard boxing ring. (Above, HistoryMiami Museum, 1963-032-60; left, author's collection.)

Hollywood Golf and Country Club, Hollywood, Florida.

In 1929, the Capone syndicate leased the Hollywood Golf and Country Club (above) located in Hollywood, Florida. Once under the syndicate's control, the country club was converted into a private gambling club that featured platinum blonde chorus girls and world-famous entertainment acts. During the day, Capone and his gang found other ways to utilize the club's vast space and amenities. When Capone's close friend, boxer Mickey Walker, was in town training for an upcoming bout, the gangster pitched a training camp behind the club's 18-hole golf course and visited daily to watch Walker train. Other boxers and friends who came to train and watch included boxers Mike Dundee (left) and Chappie Roberts (right), photographed on the Hollywood Golf and Country Club training grounds. (Both, author's collection.)

Casino operator George R.K. Carter (above left) shakes hands with sports promoter Tex Rickard (above right) after finalizing a deal to build the Miami Beach Kennel Club (below). Rickard put up $50,000 to build the racetrack and became its first president when it opened in 1929 on 1st Street and Ocean Drive. Michael Glenn, the security manager for Carl Fisher, confirmed that Capone had a controlling interest in the track and bankrolled its operation. Aside from the Kennel Club, Glenn also reported that Capone held a one-fourth interest in the Palm Island Club, a one-fourth interest in the Floridian Hotel's gambling room, and a controlling interest in Albert Bouche's Villa Venice nightclub. Following a *Miami News* editorial report linking Capone to his nightclub, Bouche sued the Miami News for $250,000 in damages. (Above, State Archives of Florida; below, HistoryMiami Museum, 1995-277-10253.)

While enjoying his new life in the Magic City, Capone still had important business to handle back in Chicago. On the top of that list was to end the war between his South Side Italian gang and the North Side Irish gang led by George "Bugs" Moran. In an attempt to wipe out Bugs Moran and his top lieutenants, Capone engineered what would be infamously referred to as the St. Valentine's Day Massacre, which took place at the SMC Cartage Company (background building with marker) on the morning of February 14, 1929. Moran escaped the fate his assassins had planned for him when the lookout in the building across the street (foreground building with marker) mistakenly identified one of the gang members as Moran. Five men, two dressed in Chicago police uniforms, entered the SMC Cartage warehouse and ordered the group of seven men to line up against the wall. At that point, the gunmen opened fire, killing six of the men instantly, with the final victim pronounced dead at the hospital a few hours later. (Author's collection.)

From left to right are massacre victims Peter Gusenberg, Albert Weinshank, Adam Heyer, John May, Reinhardt Schwimmer, and Albert Kachellek (against the wall). Frank Gusenberg was still alive when police arrived on the scene and was immediately rushed to the hospital but would provide no information on the shooters. The victims ranged from prominent members of the Moran Gang to some with little to no actual gang involvement. The Gusenberg brothers were top enforcers and muscle for the Moran Gang. Albert Weinshank managed several cleaning and dyeing operations for Moran. Adam Heyer served as the bookkeeper for the Moran Gang. John May was an occasional mechanic for the gang. Reinhardt Schwimmer was an optometrist and gangster groupie who enjoyed hanging around gangsters. Albert Kachellek, alias James Clark, was Moran's second in command. (Both, author's collection.)

On the day of the St. Valentine's Day Massacre, Capone had a morning appointment with Robert Taylor, the county solicitor of Dade County. During the hearing, Capone was asked questions regarding his relationship with Parker Henderson Jr. and his business dealings in the Miami area. He replied, "I am a gambler, play race horses." The hearing proved rather convenient for Capone, as it provided him the perfect alibi for his whereabouts during the massacre. In fact, in the days following the massacre, Capone made himself more publicly visible in Miami, looking unconcerned about the recent events in Chicago. When Capone learned that boxer Jack Sharkey was in town training for an upcoming fight against Young Stribling, he quickly arranged to visit the training grounds to watch Sharkey in action. Less than two weeks after the massacre, Capone, in rare form, allowed himself to be photographed by the press alongside sports writer Bill Cunningham (left) and boxer Jack Sharkey (right). (Author's collection.)

In the months following the St. Valentine's Day Massacre, Capone's name continually appeared in newspaper headlines across the country, connecting him to the grisly event. Shortly after his attendance at the May 1929 Atlantic City Conference (an event hosting the biggest organized crime leaders from across the country), it was decided that Capone would spend a short time in jail to appease the public and to get him out of the spotlight. (Author's collection.)

On May 16, 1930, Capone (right) and his bodyguard Frankie Rio (above) were arrested when exiting a Philadelphia movie theater. Both were charged with gun possession and sentenced to a year in prison. Upon Capone's incarceration, speculation grew as to where he would settle when he was released. Authorities across the nation made it known that Capone was persona non grata. Pictured are Capone and Rio from their Philadelphia arrest booking photos. (Author's collection.)

Capone served 10 months of his one-year prison sentence and was released on March 17, 1930. Upon Capone's release from Philadelphia's Eastern State Penitentiary, Florida governor Doyle Carlton (above), who had run for office on an antigambling platform, issued a standing order to arrest Capone on sight, escort him out of the state, and instruct him not to return. Carlton understood that Florida was more liberal than other states but vowed, "It will not be a haven for the crooks and criminals or the headquarters for gangsters and gunmen." If Capone planned to return to the Sunshine State, Carlton intended to make his stay as challenging as possible. (State Archives of Florida.)

On March 20, 1930, the Dade County Sheriff's Office and the Miami Beach Police Department raided the Capone compound at 93 Palm Avenue after receiving a report that Al Capone was spotted the previous day almost 200 miles north of Miami. Although Capone was not at the property, the police found Frankie Newton, caretaker of the residence, along with 10 sacks and three bottles of liquor, champagne, and wine. Newton, who was arrested and charged with violating the nation's Prohibition law, informed the officers that, shortly before the raid, five other men left the house for a swim in the ocean. Upon their return, waiting officers arrested Capone's brothers John and Albert, as well as Jack McGurn, Louis Cowen, and L.J. Brennan. (Both, author's collection.)

"Machine Gun" Jack McGurn was a principal member of Capone's organization and a frequent visitor to South Florida and the Capone estate. When arrested during the Palm Island raid, McGurn, who was wanted by the Chicago police, provided his name as James Vincent to evade extradition to Illinois. Ten days later, McGurn, his girlfriend Louise, and his stepbrother Anthony were arrested on a Miami golf course and searched for guns. When none were found, the officers allowed them to finish their game, then escorted Jack and Anthony to the county jail, where they were fingerprinted and photographed (right). Above, McGurn soaks up some Miami sun with his "Blonde Alibi," Louise Rolfe. (Both, John Binder Collection.)

John Capone (right), along with his cousin Chicago gangster Joseph Fischetti (center) and an unidentified friend, pose with empty liquor bottles in hand for a souvenir photograph. Unfortunately for John, the liquor bottles found in his closet during the Palm Island raid were full and resulted in a charge of illegal liquor possession. Three weeks later, John Capone was acquitted of the charges following a 10-minute deliberation from a criminal court jury. (Author's collection.)

Ralph "Bottles" Capone, dressed in his finest garb, poses for this self-commissioned publicity photograph at the famed Maurice Seymour studio in Chicago. Ralph, the most infamous Capone brother second to Al, was not present at the Palm Island raid but spent a great deal of time at the residence when visiting his brother in Miami or making a layover stop during his frequent trips to Cuba. (Author's collection.)

During the Palm Island raid, Al Capone's younger brother Albert was arrested and charged with "vagrancy," a vague charge often applied to suspected criminals who had not committed a crime. Albert paid a $500 bail and was quickly released. Following his trial, the judge ordered the case dismissed and had the bond returned to Albert. Three weeks later, while playing golf on a Miami Beach golf course, Albert was arrested again for the same offense. Below is Albert's arrest card following the raid, bearing his personal stats, signature, and fingerprints. (Right, author's collection; below, Miami-Dade County Municipal Archives.)

Following the raid on his Palm Island estate, Capone knew that, before his planned reentry into South Florida, he would need to retain legal counsel to protect him from the governor's order to eject him from the state. Capone hired attorneys James "Fritz" Gordon (left) and Vincent Giblin (below) to file a federal lawsuit to ensure him safe travels into and around the state, protected from the harassment of local and state officials. (Author's collection.)

Within a week of the filing of the lawsuit, US District Court judge Halsted Ritter entered a temporary order forbidding law enforcement from keeping Capone out of Florida and prohibiting them from "seizing, arresting, kidnapping and abusing" Capone. With the protection of the judge's order, Capone finally returned to Miami on April 20, 1930. (Notre Dame Archives.)

On the morning of May 8, 1930, just a couple of weeks after his return to Miami, Al Capone, his brother John Capone (below), Chicago alderman Albert J. Prignano, and bodyguard Nick Circella, were arrested for investigation while en route to the Olympia Theater in downtown Miami. Once taken to the police station, the harassment continued. Capone claimed he was not issued a receipt for his valuables, was refused his right to call an attorney, and was then placed in a small windowless cell with no food or water. The arrest was organized by Miami director of public safety S.D. McCreary. Once behind bars, McCreary warned Capone, "I had you arrested, and I am going to have you arrested every time you hit Miami." (Above, Miami Police Department; below, author's collection.)

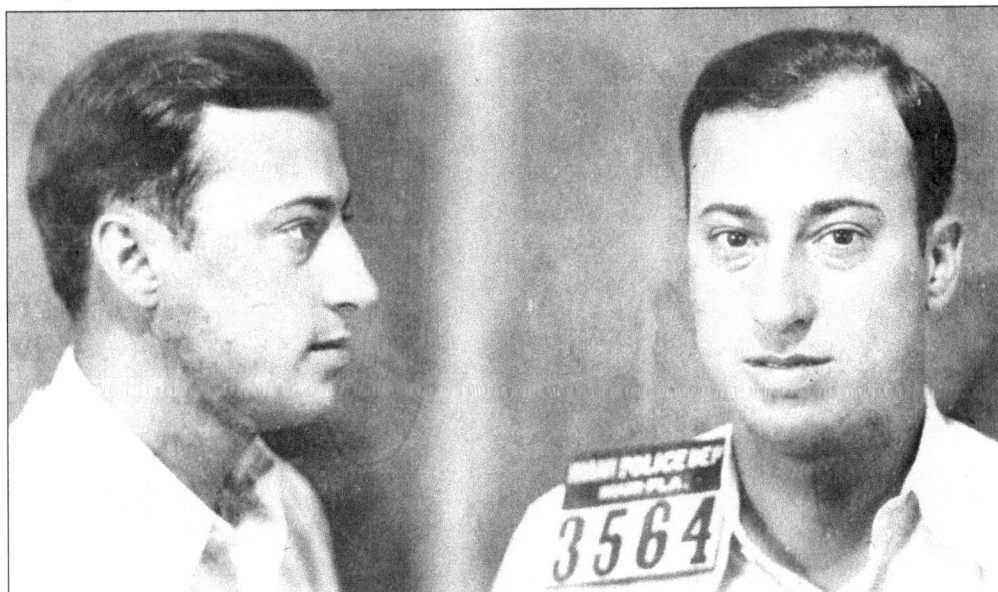

Nick Circella sullenly poses for his booking photograph after being arrested with Capone on the way to watch a matinee at the downtown Olympia Theater. Circella worked as Capone's bodyguard and was often with him or hanging around the Palm Island estate. Later in his criminal career, Nick Circella was charged with extortion and sentenced to eight years in prison for his participation in the infamous million-dollar Hollywood extortion scandal involving the Chicago Outfit. After his release from prison, Circella voluntarily left for Argentina following a deportation order. Pictured at left during better times, Circella relaxes amid Miami's white sand beaches. (Above, author's collection; left, John Binder Collection.)

Only five days after his previous arrest for investigation, Capone was arrested again on the same charge, along with three of his companions, while watching a boxing match at the American Legion Hall. Capone (left) and his cohorts were taken to the police station, where they would spend a night in jail. The next morning, all four men were released after Circuit Court Judge Uly O. Thompson issued a writ of habeas corpus stating that the city had not shown sufficient legal cause to hold the men further. However, less than a week later, Capone and one of his associates were taken into custody once again, making it the third arrest within the span of 10 days. Capone was charged with vagrancy and taken to police headquarters, where he posted a bond of $100 and was immediately released. Then, five days later, on May 24, Capone was stopped a fourth time by Miami police. On instructions from his lawyer, he refused to be taken in, and the officers left. (HistoryMiami Museum, 1989-011-19510.)

Capone continued to battle a slew of legal troubles in Miami, including a new vagrancy law aimed directly at him and the attempted padlocking of his Palm Island home. The state argued that Capone was a nuisance to his neighborhood and should be barred from entering the premises. As Capone continued to combat every charge brought against him in Miami, the US Department of Treasury began building a tax evasion case, led by US District Attorney George E.Q. Johnson (above center) and assistant DAs (from left to right) Dwight Green, Samuel G. Clawson, William J. Froelich, and Jacob Grossman. Al Capone, pictured below on the second day of his trial with his lawyers Michael Ahearn (left) and Albert Fink, was later convicted. He was sentenced to 11 years in federal prison and ordered to pay over $200,000 in back taxes. (Both, author's collection.)

On November 16, 1939, Al Capone was released from prison after serving 7.5 years of his 11-year sentence. Capone returned to his Miami Beach home, where he would reside quietly for the remainder of his life, seldom being seen in public. In this rare public appearance, Capone, photographed with his lawyer Abe Teitelbaum, attends the 1941 wedding of his son Albert "Sonny" Capone. (Author's collection.)

Albert Francis "Sonny" Capone exits St. Patrick's Church in Miami Beach with his new bride, Diana Ruth Casey Capone. Sonny Capone avoided following in his gangster dad's footsteps and led a relatively crimeless life, aside from a minor shoplifting charge in 1965 when then 45-year-old Sonny Capone was arrested after stealing $3.50 worth of batteries and aspirin from a Kwik Check Market. (Author's collection.)

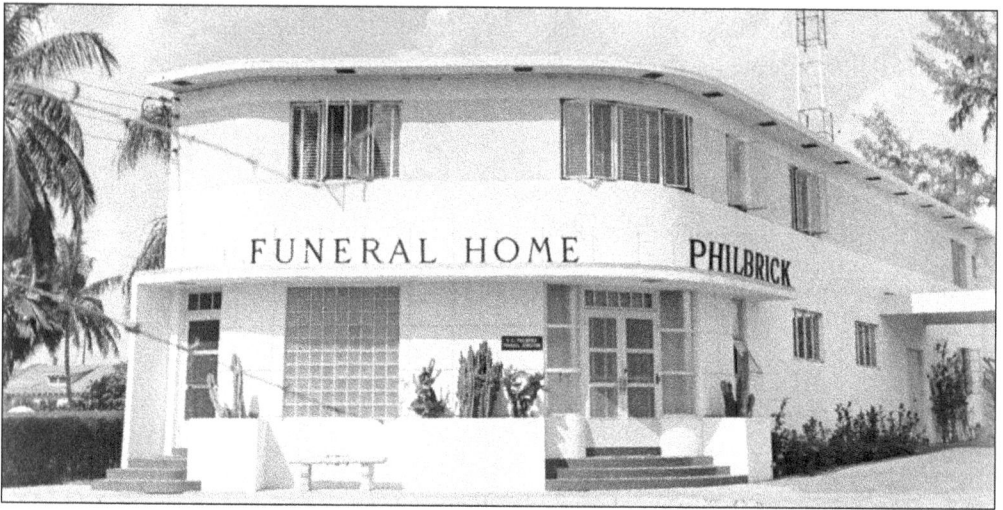

During his prison stay, Capone was diagnosed with syphilis, a disease he contracted as a young man before his marriage to Mae. By the late 1930s, Al was exhibiting signs of dementia brought on by late-stage syphilis, which in part helped secure his early release from prison and return to Miami Beach. A shell of his former self, Capone lived out his final years in declining health on his Miami property, surrounded by family and visiting friends who came to pay their respects. On January 25, 1947, Capone succumbed to his illness and passed away quietly in an upstairs bedroom of his Palm Island estate. Following his death, Capone's body was sent to Philbrick Funeral Home in Miami Beach (above) for the funeral, then returned to Chicago's Mount Olivet Cemetery for burial in the Capone family plot (below). (Both, author's collection.)

Three

BOOKIES, GAMBLERS, AND CASINOS

Throughout the history of organized crime activity in the Miami area, no endeavor was more prominent than that of illegal gambling. Bookmakers and operators controlled card games, dice games, numbers games, and any other form of gambling conceivable in establishments varying from high-end, air-conditioned casinos to hotels, restaurants, cigar stands, and beachside cabanas. Above, officers catalog seized slot machines following a 1938 gambling house raid. (HistoryMiami Museum, 1989-011-24378.)

Julian "Potatoes" Kaufman (above) started his criminal career in Chicago as a fence for stolen loot but quickly advanced to running gambling joints. In partnership with George "Bugs" Moran, Kaufman oversaw one of Chicago's most elegant casinos, the Sheridan Wave Tournament Club, until it was shut down in 1929. Leaving Chicago, Kaufman traveled to New York and then Hallandale, Florida, where he teamed up with local bookie Claude Litteral to operate a race wire service and bookmaking operation out of a large tomato-packing shed. The shed, named the Plantation, had one area stocked with craps tables and roulette wheels and another designated for bingo. Miami Beach residents and tourists trekked north into Broward County to visit the Plantation, and by the spring of 1936, Kaufman's casino had become the hottest spot in town. (Viki Varon Armstrong.)

After witnessing the success of Julian Kaufman's Plantation, New York mobster Vincent "Jimmy Blue Eyes" Alo approached Kaufman with an offer that was difficult to refuse. Alo, who was a longtime friend and partner of "mob accountant" Meyer Lansky, offered Kaufman a partnership deal where he could expand his operations while falling under the protection of the duo and their powerful associates. Once on board, Meyer Lansky, who learned how to successfully operate a gambling house in Saratoga Springs under the tutelage of Arnold "The Brain" Rothstein, began implementing his mentors' lucrative tactics into the Plantation, as well as in his quickly expanding array of casinos throughout South Florida. Improvements included the installation of kitchens, classy decor, and most important, carpet—the defining factor in what Lansky believed separated a high-class "carpet joint" from a low-end "sawdust joint." Pictured above in a private family photograph from the 1930s, Meyer Lansky poses with his two sons, Paul (left) and Buddy, while vacationing in Cuba. (Author's collection.)

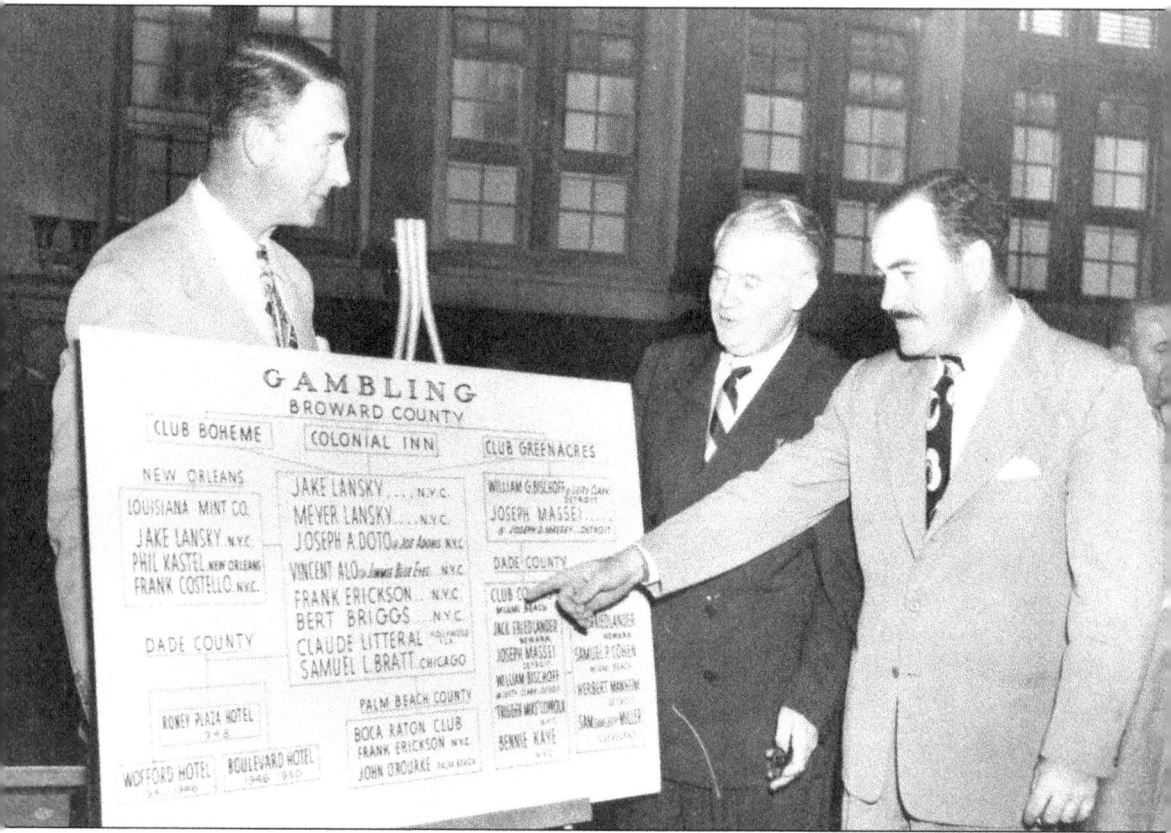

From left to right are Tennessee senator Estes Kefauver, who headed the Special Committee to Investigate Organized Crime in Interstate Commerce; Wyoming senator Lester Hunt; and Dan Sullivan, director of the Miami Crime Commission. Together, they review an intricate chart displaying the national syndicates' bookmaking operations in South Florida and the group of mobsters who operated them. Meyer Lansky and his partners were connected in one way or another to every major gambling house in southern Florida, including Club Boheme, Club Collins, Colonial Inn, Club Greenacres, the Beach Club, the Farm, and the Hollywood Yacht Club, among others. The enterprise of clubs stretched from Miami-Dade to Broward and included gambling interest in clubs as far north as Palm Beach County. (HistoryMiami Museum, 1981-099-47.)

Jake Lansky, or Jack, as he was often called, was the younger brother of Meyer Lansky and an integral part of Meyer's South Florida gambling operations. Jake arrived in Miami Beach in 1933, then moved north to Hollywood, where he was placed in the cashier cage of the Farm (formerly the Plantation). As Meyer's gambling interest expanded throughout South Florida, so did Jake's responsibilities. Jake Lansky operated the Colonial Inn, as well as a number of other casinos, on behalf of his brother Meyer and their partners Joseph Doto, Vincent Alo, Frank Costello, and Frank Erickson. Above, Jake is photographed with his daughter Roberta outside their Hollywood, Florida, home. (State Archives of Florida.)

Casino operators understood that paying off law enforcement and making contributions to local politicians was not enough to stay under the radar of the state authorities. In order to keep a successfully running operation, it was imperative to establish and maintain a favorable image within the community and to appease the residents who opposed illegal gambling. Common

gestures included charitable donations to hospitals, schools, and churches. Above, demonstrating one of these public relations tactics, Jake Lansky (far right) hands out cigars to servicemen at the Colonial Inn while hosting a dinner in their honor. (State Archives of Florida.)

Walter Clark (above center and left) was elected Broward County sheriff in 1933, and thanks to his look-the-other-way policy, gambling flourished in Broward County throughout the 1930s and 1940s. Clark admitted to knowing and accepting campaign contributions from various underworld figures but denied any knowledge of gambling taking place in the clubs around town. When pressed by the Kefauver Committee regarding his lax stance on gambling enforcement, Clark responded, "I was elected on the liberal ticket, and the people want it and they enjoy it." Besides being sheriff, Clark had his hand in a number of other businesses, most prominently the Broward Novelty Company, a cigarette vending and jukebox company that secretly operated slot machines and bolita. The company was operated in partnership with his brother Robert Clark (above right) and annually grossed over a quarter million dollars. (Above, HistoryMiami Museum, 1995-277-12181; left, State Archives of Florida.)

At the same time Sheriff Walter Clark allowed gambling to run rampant in Broward County, Dade County Sheriff Jimmy Sullivan (right) took the same wink-of-an-eye attitude while fraternizing with known gamblers and racketeers. Sullivan, or Smiling Jimmy as he was known, was elected Dade sheriff in 1944 after serving nine years as a Miami street cop, a job at which he excelled. By 1949, Sullivan's personal net worth increased from about $2,500 to well over $75,000, part of which he claimed to be unexpended political contributions. Corruption in Sullivan's office was prevalent with one deputy making enough money in four years to retire to a $26,000 farm. Three former deputy sheriffs who testified regarding corruption in their office stated they were instructed not to make any arrest related to bookmaking. Below, newly elected Jimmy Sullivan accepts the keys from retiring Sheriff D.C. Coleman. (Right, author's collection; below, HistoryMiami Museum, 1995-277-16540.)

This is Benjamin "Bugsy" Siegel's 1930 booking photograph from his Miami arrest on February 28, 1930, his 24th birthday. Siegel was arrested on gambling and vagrancy charges, for which he paid a $100 fine and was released. Aside from being a regular visitor to the Hallandale casinos operated by his childhood friends, Siegel reputedly had his hand in the bookmaking operation at the Hollywood Yacht Club along with Vincent Alo and his future Las Vegas business partner Moe Sedway. (Author's collection.)

When questioned about his involvement in Florida gambling establishments by the Kefauver Committee in 1951, Moe Sedway admitted to having an interest in the Hollywood Yacht Club, along with Julian "Potatoes" Kaufman. But when pressed further about other partners, Sedway claimed not to know their names. Sedway is pictured here at the Flamingo Hotel in Las Vegas five months after his takeover following the June 20, 1947, gangland murder of Benjamin "Bugsy" Siegel. (Author's collection.)

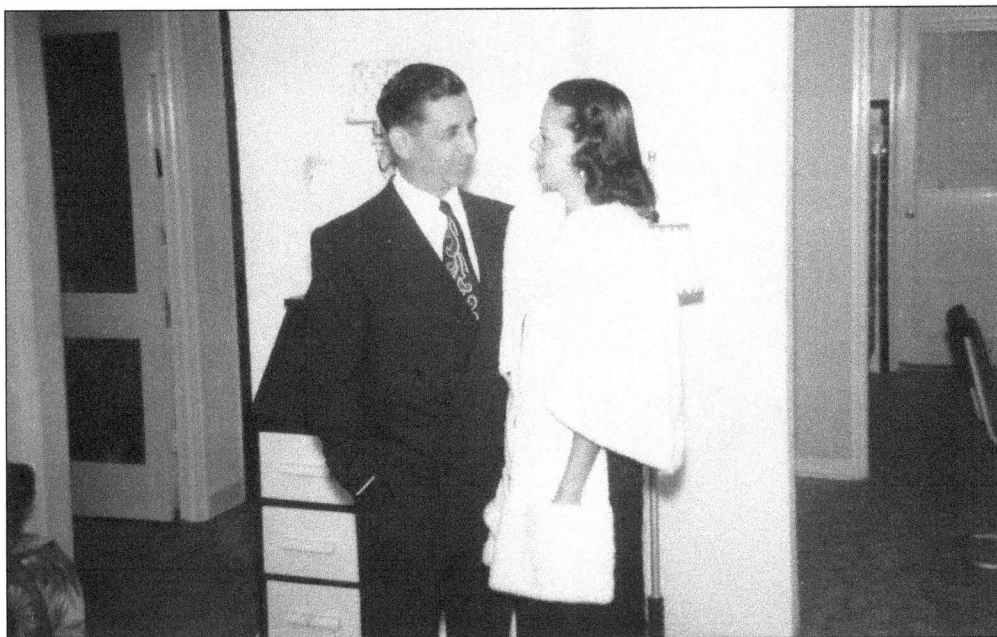

Throughout the 1930s and 1940s, Meyer Lansky continued to participate in the successful operations of his gambling establishments throughout South Florida while expanding his interest to Cuba and Las Vegas. In fact, Lansky's name was so synonymous with South Florida gambling, a stretch of Hallandale land was fondly referred to as "Lanskyland." Above, Lansky affectionately smiles at his second wife, Teddy, just months after their November 1948 wedding. The following summer, Lansky booked the five-room royal suite aboard the *Italia*, a luxury steamship, for an Italian honeymoon, where he was reunited with his longtime friend Charles "Lucky" Luciano, who was exiled to Italy after serving 10 years of his 30-year prison sentence. Below, a casually dressed Lansky enjoys a cigarette while relaxing aboard the *Italia* en route to Italy. (Both, author's collection.)

In 1940, Miami mobster Thomas Cassara took over the lease of the Wofford Hotel (above) in Miami Beach, starting a long chain of mafia involvement for the four-story beachfront hotel. The Wofford Hotel was operated in part by New York mobsters Frank Erickson and Anthony "Little Augie" Carfano, as well as brothers George and John Angersola, both high-ranking Cleveland mobsters. The hotel soon became a meeting place for well-known racketeers and gangsters from around the country. Carfano (left), who identified himself as the Wofford's managing director, was sent to Miami by Joe Adonis and Frank Costello to expand their gambling interest in the region. Besides the Wofford, Carfano would go on to hold an interest in other legitimate spas and hotels throughout Miami Beach. (Both, author's collection.)

Frank Erikson (right) was arguably the largest bookmaker in the country, with betting agents representing his interest in every major city in the United States. During the early 1940s, Erickson used Miami Beach's Wofford Hotel as a base of operations for the handling of large layoff bets or money received by him in New York, New Jersey, and other cities. Erickson's ownership of South Florida gambling establishments was often in the name of his attorney, Abe Allenberg; however, when his Park Avenue office was raided in May 1949, business records in a folder labeled "Florida" exposed his true gambling interest and underworld links. Erickson's partners were revealed to be New York mob boss Frank Costello, pictured below with his wife, and Joseph Adonis, Costello's close ally who identified himself in Florida as Costello's nephew. (Both, author's collection.)

In 1939, Eliot Ness, former famed Prohibition agent, conducted a major investigation into Cleveland's numbers racket, causing an exodus of mobsters to flee to Miami to avoid prosecution. Six of the indicted men boarded the *Wood Duck*, a yacht belonging to Continental Press owner Arthur McBride, and traveled through the Great Lakes, passing down the inland waterway to the Miami area. (Author's collection.)

Among the group arriving by boat were George "King" Angersola (above) and his brother John "Johnny King" Angersola (right), both prominent members of the Cleveland Mafia. Once in Miami, the Angersola brothers established illegal gambling operations on behalf of the Cleveland mob, with shared interest in the Wofford, Grand, and Carib Hotels, as well as high-stakes, on-premise gambling. (Author's collection.)

In 1946, Philadelphia bookmaker and horse book operator Dave Glass, along with fellow horse book operator Bennie Street, took over the lease of the Sands Hotel in Miami Beach with a required deposit of $90,000. After their acquisition, the hotel quickly became a hotbed for gamblers, racketeers, and gangsters, especially those from the Philadelphia group headed by Harry "Nig Rosen" Stromberg. (Author's collection.)

Harry "Nig Rosen" Stromberg was a New York native who moved to Philadelphia during the Prohibition era and established himself there as the kingpin of the underworld. Following the end of Prohibition, Rosen and his predominantly Jewish gang needed new sources of revenue and began setting up gambling operations across the country. During winter months, the Rosen mob utilized the Sands Hotel in Miami Beach as their gambling headquarters. (Author's collection.)

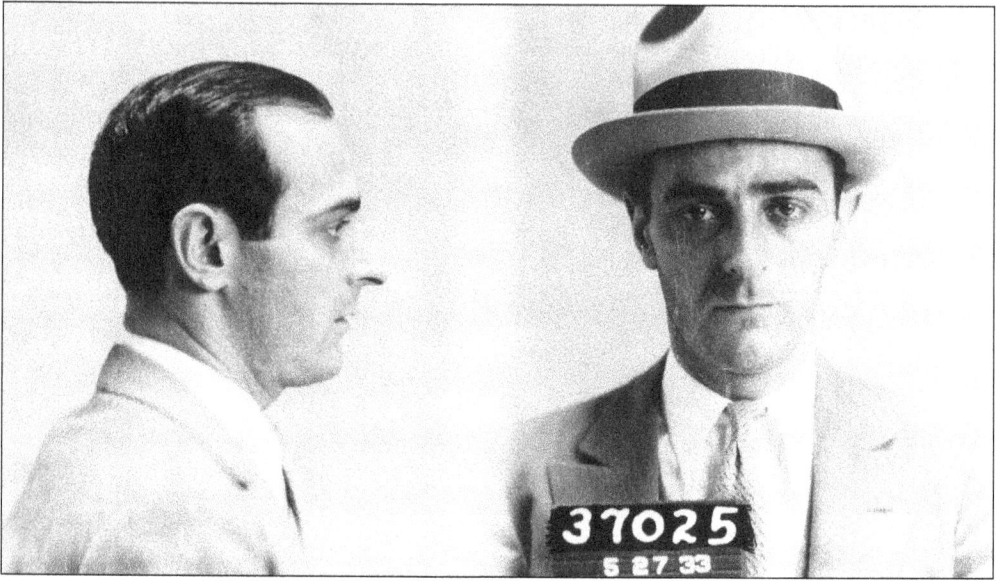

Operating out of the Sands and Grand Hotels during the winter season, Max "Willie" Weisberg (above) served as the chief lieutenant for the Nig Rosen mob and overseer of the gang's gambling interest in Miami Beach. Weisberg, operating with other Rosen gang members, such as Max "Chinkie" Rothman and Rosen's brother Nathan "Nussie Rosen" Stromberg, reported back to their gang chief, who was located in New York City. Samuel "Cappie" Hoffman (below) was Weisberg's bodyguard and chief enforcer, assisting in the gang's continued successful gambling operations. Throughout Pennsylvania and New Jersey, Hoffman was arrested 18 times for offenses ranging from bookmaking to murder. Tired of Hoffman's continued arrest and their futile attempts to lock him up, the Philadelphia police ran him out of town, at which point he settled in Miami Beach. (Both, author's collection.)

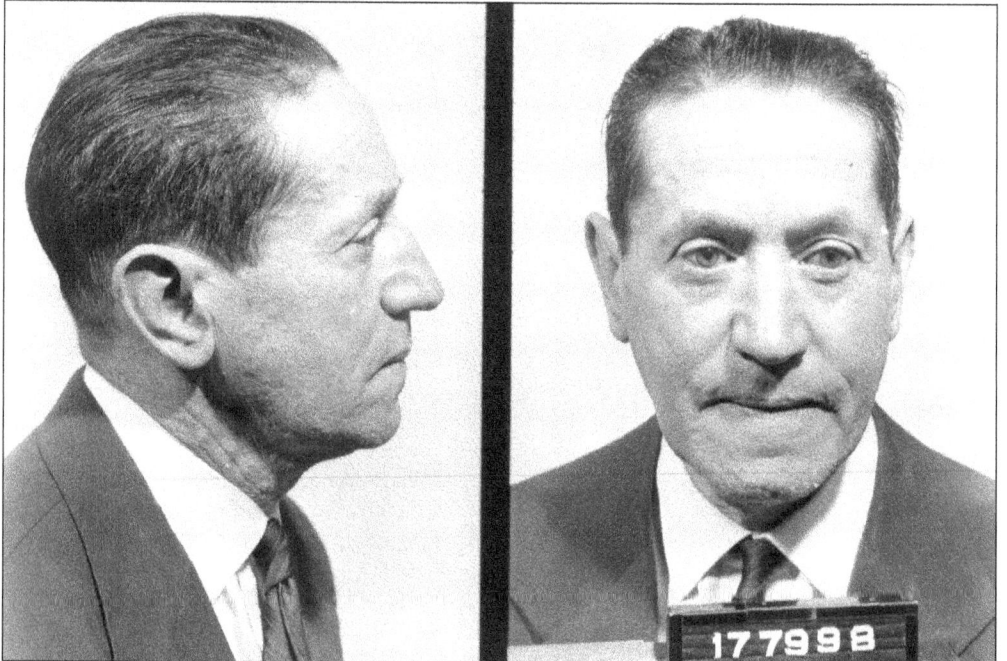

During a 1949 weekly radio broadcast, Daniel P. Sullivan, director of the Crime Commission of Greater Miami, announced the newest arrivals to the Miami gambling scene. Included on the list were the Newman Brothers, who Sullivan warned "are wise to the way of crime whether it be in an organized racket or through stick-ups, burglaries or robberies." Moe Newman (above) was a strong-arm man for the Nig Rosen mob, while his brother Jack (below) was one of the gang's chief executioners. Before his arrival in Miami Beach, Jack Newman and Al Silverberg were the prime suspects in the 1930 murder of Prohibition agent John G. Finiello, who was shot and killed during a New Jersey brewery raid. Newman was never tried because of witness identification problems, but in 1932, he received a life sentence for a mob hit, for which he served only 16 years. (Both, author's collection.)

Marco "Small Man" Reginelli was a New Jersey mobster with an interest in the Nig Rosen mob's gambling operations at the Sands Hotel. During a 1942 trip to Miami, Reginelli purchased an airline ticket for his girlfriend, Louise Abate, to join him in the Magic City. After a 10-day vacation, Reginelli was indicted under the federal Mann Act, which made it a felony to transport any woman for the purpose of prostitution, debauchery, or any other immoral purpose. Although Abate was a consenting adult female, Reginelli refused to answer questions about their accused improper relations and was ultimately convicted and denied naturalization as a US citizen. (Author's collection.)

After avoiding a murder charge due to insufficient evidence, Detroit gangster Joseph Massei (above) migrated to Miami around 1935 and, along with fellow Detroit native William "Lefty Clark" Bischoff, held a majority interest in Club Greenacres. The bulk income from the club was generated from what was known as the "Big Game" or the "New York craps game," which was financed by Massei and controlled by Clark, a skilled craps operator. Operating from a penthouse suite in Miami Beach's Grand Hotel, Massei soon opened the Miami Provisions Co., a produce and grocery delivery service that served as a front for his illegal businesses and delivered to almost every major hotel and resort in the city. In the 1950s, following his Miami gambling ventures, Lefty Clark went on to operate the plush new casino at the Tropicana in Havana (right). (Both, author's collection.)

"They're Off", Tropical Park, Miami, Florida

374

In 1941, the majority of the Tropical Park racetrack, located near Coral Gables, was controlled by Owney Madden, former leading underworld figure in Prohibition-era Manhattan who relocated to Hot Springs, Arkansas, in 1935. Between Madden's wife, his brother's brother-in-law, and close associate Frenchy Fox, Madden owned 51 percent of the track's stock, all of which was controlled by a trust agreement established by his wife's uncle. Another 20 percent belonged to New York gambler Frank Erickson in the name of his front man Abe Allenberg, while another percentage was owned by a Chicago investor believed to be fronting for Chicago mob boss Frank Nitti. Above, this 1943 Tropical Park postcard was sent to Madden, with the reverse bearing horse names for an upcoming race. Below, Owney Madden pours drinks for friends at a mock saloon in Hot Springs, Arkansas. (Above, author's collection; below, Marnix Brendel, www.headsofthefamily.com.)

Four

THE S&G SYNDICATE

Operating under the protection of the Miami Beach Police Department and the Dade County Sheriff's Office, the S&G Syndicate controlled bookmaking and race wire operations throughout Miami Beach with little to no outside interference. Seen here is an interior view of a standard S&G bookmaking operation where bookies, using phone banks to connect with racetracks nationwide, would gather the latest results to provide bettors with the most accurate, up-to-the-minute information. (HistoryMiami Museum, 1989-011-6100.)

In 1944, local independently operating bookmakers Jules Levitt, Sam Cohen, Eddie Rosenbaum, Harold Savley, and Charles Friedman agreed to eliminate competition among themselves and formed the S&G Corporation, a company in which they pooled their resources and financed other bookies throughout Miami. Within four years of operation, the syndicate held a dominant grip on all race wire and bookmaking operations in Miami Beach, controlling concessions at over 200

hotels, cabanas, cigar stores, and other high-traffic locations. According to their financial books, the syndicate grossed over $26.5 million in bets—a figure the federal government contended was substantially below its true gross. Pictured at a 1950 Senate crime investigation hearing in Washington, DC, are, from left to right, Jules Levitt, syndicate lawyer Ben Cohen, Eddie Rosenbaum, Harold Savley, and office cashier Leo Levitt. (HistoryMiami Museum, 1995-277-17394.)

Edward Rosenbaum, active manager for the S&G Syndicate, maintained a plush executive office in the Mercantile Bank Building near Lincoln Road, where the daily collections from bookmakers were received, financial records were stored, and the occasional accounting of their books was performed. Meanwhile, occupying a penthouse office atop a Midtown Miami Hotel, telephones connecting to all parts of the country, from California to New York, made it possible to constantly check on bets from the biggest racetracks across the country. Within the penthouse office, up-to-the-minute racing news would pour in over the race wire, and the results would be distributed to smaller branch offices throughout Miami Beach. These branch offices allowed the syndicate to receive information from their bookies, who, in turn, could receive information from the wire service. (HistoryMiami Museum, 1995-277-15930.)

A nattily attired Jules Levitt appears for a hearing regarding his involvement with S&G, a gambling syndicate with more than 200 independent bookmakers operating under its umbrella. Bookies would negotiate a price to run a concession within a hotel or other location and then paid the agreed-upon amount from their own pockets. As customers placed bets, bookies would call them into a local branch office, and at the end of the day, they would either deposit their winnings with the branch or, on rare occasions when losses exceeded winnings, pick up cash to pay off winners. Then, on either a monthly or seasonal basis, total profits were calculated, minus certain expenses paid by the bookie, and the remainder was split evenly between the bookie and S&G. From his profits, a bookie would pay a weekly fee up to $150 for the race wire results and operating expenses. (HistoryMiami Museum, 1995-277-17389.)

Charles Friedman, visibly annoyed by press photographers, appears in court to answer questions regarding S&G. Besides their tremendous gambling income, S&G members made numerous and extremely profitable real estate transactions with the assistance of the city attorney. After purchasing oceanfront property, the attorney would file for rezoning, switching it from residential to hotel/apartment zoning. Once approved, the syndicate would sell the property and triple their profits. (HistoryMiami Museum, 1995-277-14093.)

S&G founding member Sam Cohen is photographed here while exiting a courthouse in downtown Miami. Sam's brother Ben Cohen was an attorney who worked exclusively for the syndicate and often appeared and argued cases on behalf of any of the more than 200 bookmakers who happened to be arrested. If needed, the syndicate would pay the bookies' fines and arrange bail so they could resume operations. (HistoryMiami Museum, 1995-277-12359.)

The Roney Plaza Hotel in Miami Beach (above) was an ideal location for any ambitious bookie. In 1949, gambler Frank Erickson of the New York Syndicate leased a three-month bookie concession at the hotel for $45,000. The concession was previously leased by an S&G bookie, but hotel owner J. Myer Schine later testified that he wanted someone who would run it professionally, responsibly, and quietly, so he turned to Erickson. Detective Pat Perdue urged Schine to return the concession to S&G, but when Schine declined the request, Erickson's operation at the Roney Plaza was raided and shut down. The following season, the bookie concession was leased back to the S&G Syndicate. Below is the famous poolside cabana club at the Roney Plaza where bookies set up shop and a large portion of illegal revenue was collected. (Both, author's collection.)

Chicago gangster Harry "Muscle" Russell proved the validity of his aforementioned nickname in January 1949 when he, acting on behalf of the Chicago Outfit, approached the S&G Syndicate about becoming a one-sixth partner in the $26-million-a-year bookmaking operation with a buy-in of only $20,000. The syndicate refused his proposal and immediately began feeling the repercussions when their betting locations were suddenly raided by Dade County sheriff Jimmy Sullivan and Florida governor's special investigator W.O. Crosby. At about the same time of the raids, the Continental Press Service, controlled by the Chicago mob, cut off S&G from the wire service, denying them of race results and forcing them to shut down operations for a period of two weeks. Left with no choice, S&G accepted Russell as a full partner, at which point the raids ceased and the wire service resumed. (Author's collection.)

Daniel P. Sullivan, a former FBI agent who assisted in tracking down notorious outlaws like John Dillinger and the Barker-Karpis gang, left the bureau in 1942 and moved to Miami to apply his skills in the private security industry. By the late 1940s, Sullivan had become the leading authority on combating organized crime in Miami, compiling files on all the large criminal groups operating throughout southeast Florida, including the biggest of them all—the S&G Syndicate. In 1948, Sullivan became the founding director of the Greater Miami Crime Commission, whose main objective was to inform the public of open gambling and corruption within their city. During his crusade, Sullivan organized a series of radio broadcasts in which he singled out individual gambling operators, often S&G members, and exposed their illegal activities throughout the community. Above, Sullivan poses for a 1970 studio photograph as the executive vice president of the Crime Commission of Greater Miami. (Author's collection.)

Daniel P. Sullivan and Melvin J. Richard (left), a no-nonsense Miami Beach city councilman who refused payoffs from the syndicate, set their sights on eliminating illegal gambling and bringing down the S&G Syndicate. Using other politicians they had in their pocket, the syndicate tried to oust Richard from his councilman seat, but the issue was thrown out once it reached the Florida Supreme Court. In 1950, Sullivan and Richard appeared before the Kefauver Committee (below) to testify regarding the iron grip the syndicate held on Miami Beach politicians and the law enforcement that allowed corruption and vice to run rampant along the Gold Coast. Following the three-day televised hearing, S&G members could not escape the exposure, and the syndicate was soon dismantled. Tired of the constant harassment and need to defend their reputation, all five members eventually left Miami. (Left, HistoryMiami Museum, 1984-001-134-30; below, author's collection.)

Five

SWIMMING WITH THE FISHES

By 1950, the American mafia had fully infiltrated South Florida, with active members from every major crime family representing their organization's interest. With the warm waters tested and approved by their earlier-arriving contemporaries, mobsters eager for a piece of the action flocked to South Florida for business, vacation, and for many, the establishment of a winter or permanent residence. At right, during a fishing trip to Miami, FBI chief J. Edgar Hoover poses smilingly with a sailfish, which was later mounted and displayed in his DC office for the remainder of his career. (Author's collection.)

The Fischetti brothers (left to right: Charlie, Rocco, and Joseph), pictured on Miami Beach, were high-ranking members of the Chicago Outfit and first cousins of Al Capone, for whom they served as bodyguards and chauffeurs in their early years. In addition to operating some of the biggest illegal gambling clubs in Illinois, the brothers were close friends with Frank Sinatra and escorted the entertainer to Cuba in December 1946 to meet with Charlie "Lucky" Luciano during the infamous Havana Conference. Below, pictured at Charlie's Miami Beach home, Rocco (left) and Charlie enjoy a sunny afternoon lunch with their mother (center) and various female members of the family. (Both, author's collection.)

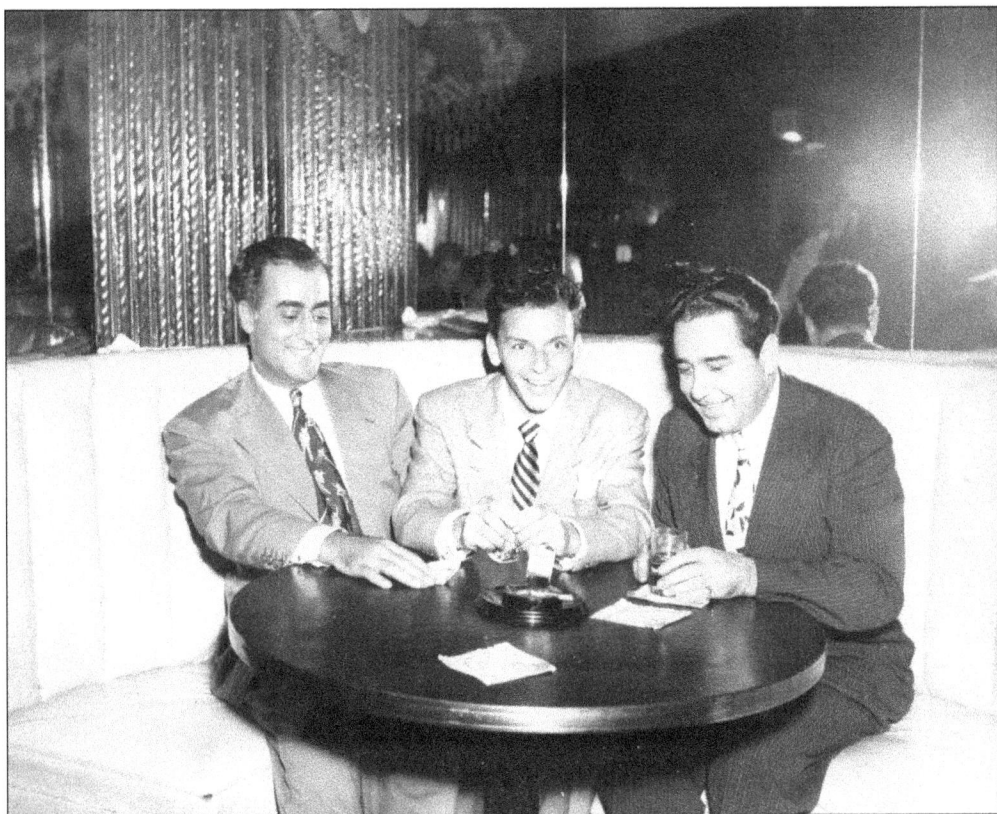

Joseph Fischetti (left) and Frank Sinatra (center), pictured above with an unidentified man at the famous Copacabana nightclub, shared a close friendship that endured over three decades. In the early 1950s, Fischetti moved to Miami Beach and concocted an arrangement between Sinatra, the Fontainebleau Hotel, and himself, offering an annual two-week singing engagement of Sinatra in return for the position of a talent scout at the hotel. Varying reports claim that Fischetti was paid between $500 and $1,000 a week for his new position in which he would often call on his crooning crony for help acquiring new talent acts to perform. Below, Sinatra and Fischetti are pictured standing aboard a boat with two unidentified men. (Both, author's collection.)

Handwritten on photograph: *Blue Fin Tuna* / WEIGHT 505 / LENGTH 8 feet 8in / May 16 1948 / Time 45 m

In addition to his role as a talent scout at the Fontainebleau Hotel, Joseph Fischetti, according to police files, also ran the hotel's card room, where high-stakes card games and well-financed craps games were routinely organized. To mask his profits from the Fontainebleau card room, Fischetti put up the money to open Puccini's Restaurant on 79th Street, a venture in which Frank Sinatra allegedly held a small interest. However, official documents reveal that the restaurant was owned, at least on paper, by Thomas and Marie Monaco, Fischetti's sister and brother-in-law. Above, Joey Fischetti shows off his trophy catch, a 500-pound bluefin tuna, after a day out fishing in the Atlantic Ocean. (Author's collection.)

72

As Joseph Fischetti established himself as a trusted mobster in Miami Beach, an important function in his underworld duties consisted of serving as a liaison for high-ranking mafia figures visiting the Magic City. Fischetti, seen above with his showgirl girlfriend Willetta Stellmacher, escorted guests around upon their arrival and introduced them to influential locals and business associates. Police documents confirm that whenever investigators attempted to locate underworld characters in Miami, Fischetti possessed the power to locate the subject in question. (Author's collection.)

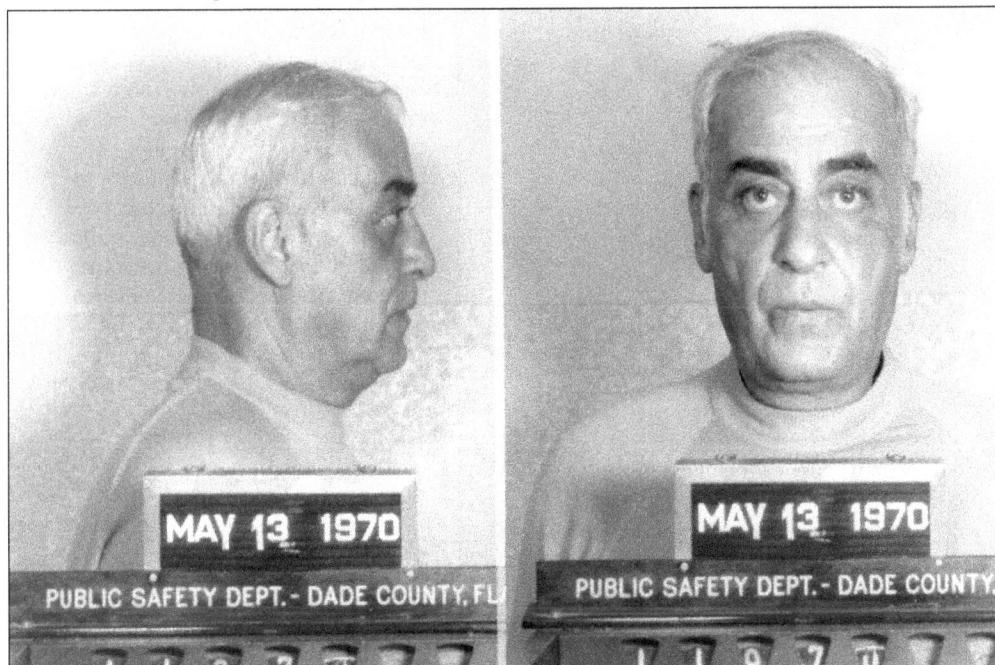

Although Joseph Fischetti's rap sheet dated back to 1932, his only conviction came in 1970 when he and Donald Gillette, secretary-treasurer and business agent of Teamsters Local 769, were sentenced to six months in jail, a $4,000 fine, and one year of probation for accepting a $15,900 payoff to destroy a labor contract. The two men accepted the bribe from Maurice Bellows, a Miami builder who received immunity for his testimony against Fischetti and Gillette. (Author's collection.)

Unlike his brothers Charlie and Joseph, Rocco Fischetti never established a permanent residence in South Florida but often visited when taking a break from his successful operation of some of the biggest illegal gambling establishments in Illinois on behalf of the Chicago Outfit. Rocco's name occasionally turned up in connection with his brothers' Miami business ventures, but for Rocco, Miami was simply a destination to escape the pressures of the Windy City. (Author's collection.)

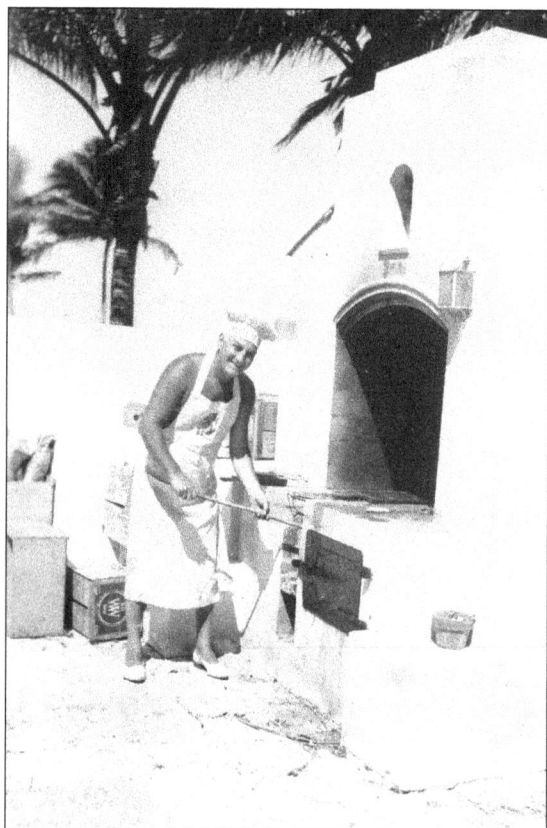

In these private family photographs, Rocco Fischetti enjoys the Magic City and the vast activities its warm climate offers. Above, the Fischetti family plays baseball, with Rocco at bat and his kid sister in the background playing catcher. At left, attired in chef's hat and apron, Rocco tends to a homemade pizza in his brother's custom-built backyard brick oven. (Author's collection.)

Martin Accardo (right), brother of Chicago mob boss Anthony Accardo, was sentenced to a one-year imprisonment following a conviction for his refusal to answer any questions during a Senate crime investigation hearing regarding his association with the *Miami Beach Morning Mail* newspaper. Accardo spent $125,000 financing the newspaper, which served as a liberal public voice for the mob's activities in South Florida. Within its first month of operation, the *Miami Beach Morning Mail* published editorials speaking favorably about gambling in Miami and lauded such figures as New York crime boss Frank Costello. After only 48 days of operation, the *Miami Beach Morning Mail* ceased publication. Below, acknowledging only his name, Accardo is photographed stubbornly declining questions "on grounds that I might incriminate myself." (Author's collection.)

Accompanied by his niece Marion (left) and daughter Antoinette (right), Chicago mob boss Sam "Mooney" Giancana gazes lovingly at his wife, Angelina, while enjoying dinner and a show at Ciro's nightclub in Miami Beach. Giancana was a frequent guest of the Magic City but made his most historic visits in the fall of 1960. According to declassified documents, CIA agent Robert Maheu approached Giancana, Santo Trafficante Jr., and Johnny Roselli about a plot to assassinate Fidel Castro. Meeting at the Fontainebleau Hotel, the men discussed the best method for eliminating Castro and decided on poisoning his food or drink. Following their meeting, the CIA provided "six pills of high lethal content" but backed out after an initial assassin got cold feet. The operation was canceled, and no further attempts were made. (Author's collection.)

Dave Yaras, a Chicago hit man with strong connections to mob bosses Sam Giancana and Santo Trafficante Jr., is seen here in a Dade County Public Safety Department identification photograph. Yaras was also closely associated with Teamsters union president Jimmy Hoffa and helped establish the Teamster Local 320 in Miami, where Trafficante held an office to run his illegal activities. On February 11, 1962, a planted FBI microphone in a Miami mob hangout revealed a disturbing conversation between Davie Yaras and Chicago mobsters Jackie Cerone, Fifi Buccieri, and Jimmy Torello. In the conversation, all parties discussed the proposed kidnapping and killing of Chicago Union boss Frank Esposito, who was vacationing in Miami at the time. The three gangsters pragmatically debated the best method of execution, with suggestions including an axe at their hangout, a knife in a car, or an invitation out on a boat to alleviate the inconvenience of disposal. After plotting the murder, the gangsters sat around and fondly discussed some of their favorite personal past hits. Esposito's life was spared when the FBI notified the Florida authorities of the murder plan. (Author's collection.)

Jimmy Hoffa, who used the Eden Roc Hotel as his campaign headquarters, celebrates his overwhelming victory with a congratulatory kiss from his wife, Josephine, after being elected the new International Brotherhood of Teamsters (IBT) president at the 1957 Miami convention. Hoffa had a long history with organized crime figures dating back to his early labor union days in Detroit—a connection that likely led to his disappearance on July 30, 1975. (Author's collection.)

New Jersey mobster Anthony "Tony Pro" Provenzano was a onetime close associate of Hoffa and former vice president of the Teamsters union. Following a fallout between the two, Provenzano was a top suspect in the disappearance of Jimmy Hoffa and, after initial questioning in the case, quickly fled to his Hallandale, Florida, home to avoid further interrogation. Provenzano is seen here with a young relative after a day of fishing in Haulover. (Marnix Brendel, www.headsofthefamily.com.)

Michael "Trigger Mike" Coppola was a New York mobster who operated the Harlem policy racket (formerly belonging to Dutch Schultz) in the 1930s and 1940s. Around 1950, Coppola purchased a home on Miami's Alton Road and continued his gambling operations, including bankrolling bookies from a poolside cabana at the Fontainebleau Hotel. Following a short 1960s prison stint, Coppola quietly lived out the remainder of his life in his Alton Road home. (Author's collection.)

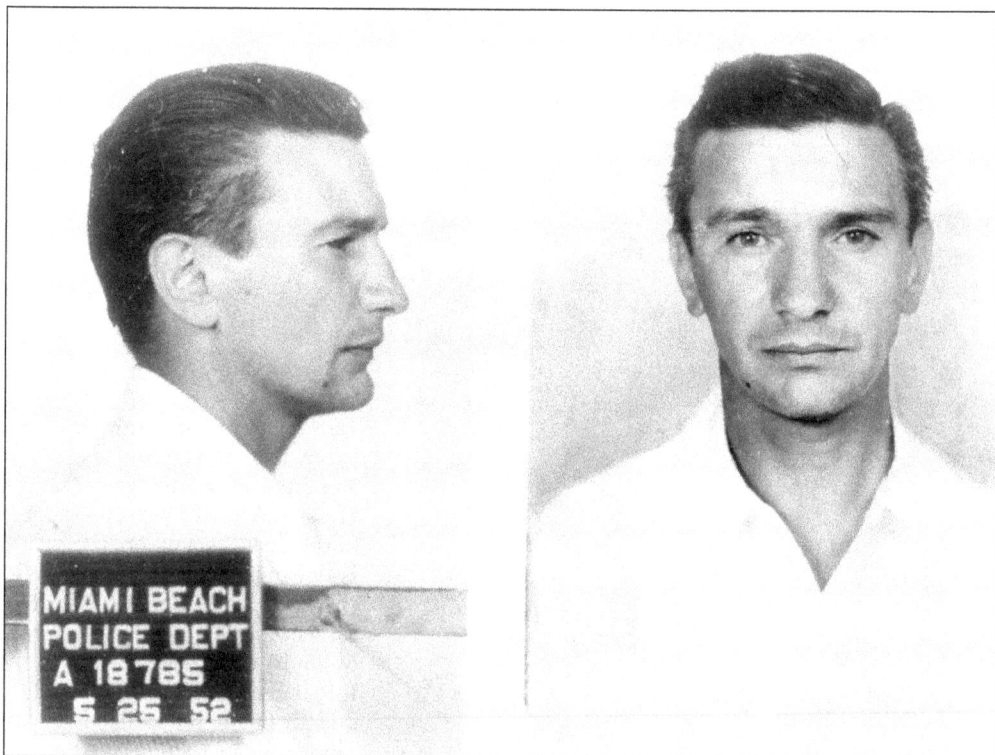

Pasquale "Patsy" Erra was a bantamweight boxer with high hopes and a winning record until his arrest for larceny and subsequent prison sentence. Upon his release, Erra began working for Trigger Mike Coppola and eventually became his chief enforcer, following him to Miami Beach in the 1950s. Along with Vincent Teriaca, Erra owned Johnina Hotel's Dream Bar on 71st Street and was regarded as a highly connected Miami Beach gangster. (Author's collection.)

Frankie "The Wop" Carbo was a New York mobster and former gunman for the Brooklyn-based hit squad Murder Incorporated. Having avoided prosecution on more than five murder charges, Carbo settled in Miami and began working as a boxing promoter, manager, and fight-fixer, which earned him the reputation as the "underworld's czar of boxing." Of most significance, Carbo and his partner, Frank "Blinky" Palermo, owned a majority interest in heavyweight boxer Sonny Liston, who later won the World Heavyweight Championship in 1962. Carbo was eventually convicted of managing boxers without a license and, in 1961, was sentenced to 25 years in prison for conspiracy and extortion against welterweight boxer Don Jordan. Confiscated as evidence by the NYPD, this receipt for $200 was sent to boxer Walter "Popeye" Woods from Carbo while operating out of Miami Beach's Dempsey-Vanderbilt Hotel. (Both, author's collection.)

Louis Nash arrived in Miami Beach in the mid-1950s following a series of arrests in New York and Ohio. Within 10 years, Nash became a leading shylock in Miami Beach, which led to a partnership with Ettore Coco, a high-ranking, Miami-based New York City mobster who at one time served as the acting boss of the Lucchese crime family. (Miami-Dade County Municipal Archives.)

In 1972, Nash, Coco, and Coco's brother-in-law James Falco were arrested on loan-sharking charges, with Nash receiving an additional separate charge for possession of $60,000 worth of stolen television tubes. One victim testified that after receiving a $12,000 loan from Falco, interest alone totaled $27,000, and threats of injury were common if the $300 weekly payments were not made on time. The trio was sentenced to 15 years in prison for loan-sharking and extortion. (Miami-Dade County Municipal Archives.)

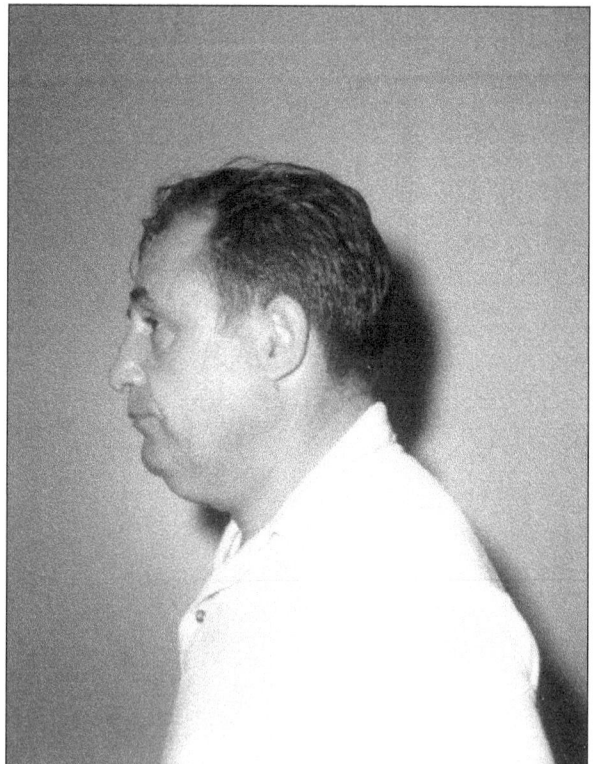

Alfred "The Owl" Polizzi (right) was a Cleveland mobster who began purchasing South Florida real estate in the late 1930s. By the mid-1940s, following a short prison stint for failure to pay liquor taxes, Polizzi had become a permanent resident, settling into the quiet city of Coral Gables. Working alongside the Cleveland mobsters who preceded him to Miami, Polizzi made his money in gambling and invested his illegal profits in the Thompson-Polizzi Construction Co. (below). Although opened as a front for Polizzi's illegal business activities, the Thompson-Polizzi Construction Co. became a prominent general contractor within the community and eventually built up a large part of Coral Gables, including Catholic schools, clubhouses, theaters, and posh homes for his mobster friends. (Both, HistoryMiami Museum; right, 1995-277-15497; below, 1995-277-15496.)

Thomas J. McGinty (right), better known as "Blackjack" McGinty for his involvement in gambling establishments, is pictured with Massachusetts senator and future president John F. Kennedy at an event on January 28, 1956. After a failed boxing career, McGinty began promoting and operating gambling clubs throughout Cleveland, where he became one of the city's largest bootleggers until his arrest and conviction in 1924. After his release, McGinty involved himself in syndicate gambling operations that spanned the nation, including Carter's, a Miami Beach casino that local newspapers described as "the biggest gambling establishment from a standpoint of money handled that had ever been operated in the United States since the days of the Gold Rush." McGinty, representing Cleveland partners Moe Dalitz, Morris Kleinman, Lou Rothkopf, and Sam Tucker, owned 65 percent of Carter's, while William Schwartz held a 25 percent interest on behalf of the New York mob. The remaining 10 percent was owned by Carter's developer and former Capone business partner George Carter. (Author's collection.)

In 1950, the State of Ohio closed McGinty's largest Cleveland gambling establishment, the Mound's Club. The following year, McGinty was subpoenaed to testify before Senator Kefauver's committee on organized crime. McGinty escaped federal prosecution and, shortly thereafter, moved to West Palm Beach, Florida, where he used his illegal profits from gambling to invest in real estate throughout South Florida. Above, Thomas McGinty (left) poses with wife Helen and another couple outside the exclusive Lake Shore Club near Palm Beach, Florida. Below, McGinty and his wife pose with associates at the Las Vegas Desert Inn, where McGinty invested $150,000 for a 7.1 percent share. (Both, author's collection.)

Morris Barney Dalitz, better known as "Moe" Dalitz, started his criminal career as a Cleveland bootlegger during Prohibition but would ultimately be remembered as one of the founding fathers of modern-day Las Vegas, holding an interest in the Desert Inn and the Stardust Casino. Before being dubbed "Mr. Las Vegas," Dalitz owned shares in gambling establishments across the nation, including the Frolics Club in Miami. Additionally, Dalitz and his Cleveland syndicate partners Morris Kleinman, Thomas McGinty, and Sam Tucker had a controlling financial interest in the Harbor Island Spa Hotel in North Bay Village. Besides his lucrative business ventures, Dalitz annually visited Miami during the winter and often anchored his yacht at the Harbor Island Spa Hotel. Here, Moe Dalitz, with tools in hand, improves the motor's efficiency aboard the *Moby Dick* while preparing for a yachting excursion in the Mediterranean. (Author's collection.)

Six

BOLITA AND THE CUBAN REVOLUTION

Following the exposure of the 1950 Kefauver Committee, Miami mobsters relocated their gambling operations, most notably to Cuba and Las Vegas. Throughout the 1950s, former Miami gamblers made millions under the leadership of Cuban dictator Fulgencio Batista until his leadership was overthrown by Fidel Castro and the Cuban Revolution, prompting tens of thousands of Cubans to flee to Miami (right), where a new group of gamblers were eager to capitalize on the Cuban lottery game known as bolita. (Author's collection.)

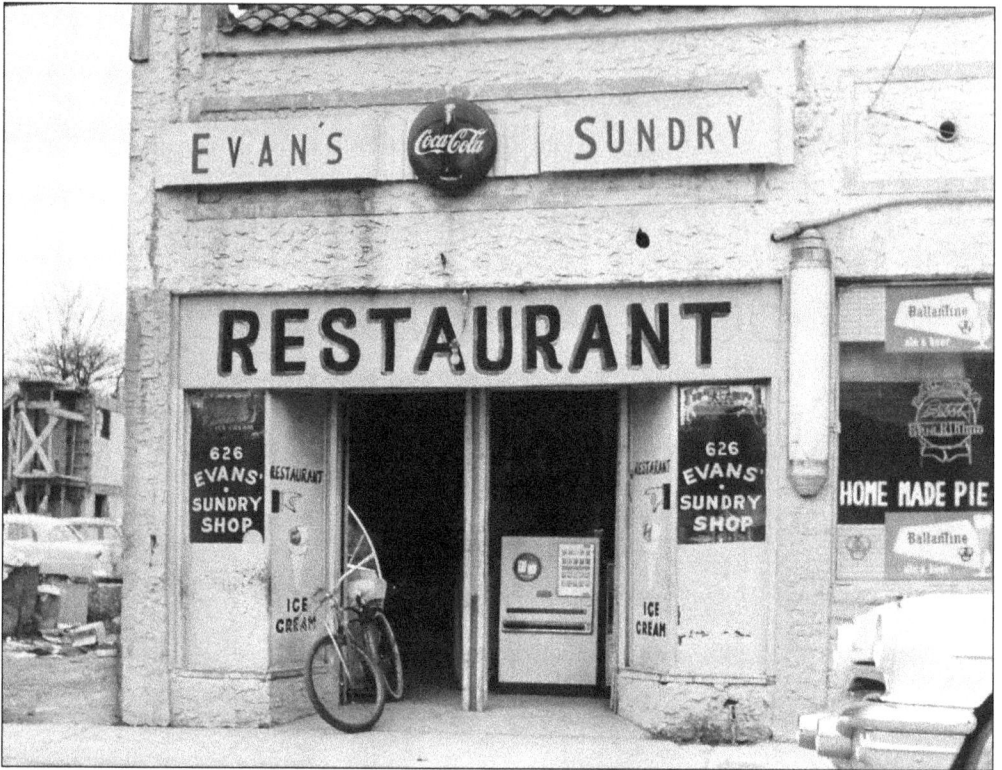

Although illegal, purchasing bolita tickets was no hard feat and could be accomplished by providing numbers over the counter at almost any small café or convenience store in low-income neighborhoods. The game was most popular within the working-class Hispanic, Italian, and African American population, where a bet of just 25¢ could result in winning up to $250. Evan's Sundry Shop (above), located in Miami's Overtown District, was one of the four shops discovered upon a brief hunt by ambitious *Miami Herald* reporter Dom Bonafede, who strolled in without hesitation and purchased four bolita tickets, no questions asked. In the previous week, Bonafede visited Al's Cash Market (below) and reported, "Al's Cash Market specializes in meat and numbers, where bolita is sold side by side with baloney." (Both, author's collection.)

Bolita was similar to other number rackets, with the main difference being that the winning numbers were selected on premise in a twice-daily drawing. The usual procedure consisted of an operator opening a wooden case to reveal 100 individually numbered balls. Bettors were allowed to view the balls and ensure no duplicates existed. From there, an operator would place the balls in a cloth bag, shake it several times, and then toss the bag to a designated catcher who would catch not the bag but one of the balls through the cloth. The selected ball would then be "tied off" in the corner of the bag, final bets would be collected, and the winning ball would be revealed. Bettors could increase their odds with a parlay made possible by the drawing of two additional balls. Another variant, named Policy, consisted of placing balls numbered 1 to 78 in the bag, with the catcher drawing 12 balls. To win, a bettor needed 3 of the 12 numbers, for which they would collect $9 for each nickel bet. (HistoryMiami Museum, 1989-011-6119.)

SAT., MAY 7, '49

A C E   DRAW 146
BELMONT PARK, N.Y.

Total
3 Races: 125.20

Total
5 Races: 174.00

Total
7 Races: 237.10

TODAY'S
NUMBER   547

Number Must
Correspond With
NY Daily Racing
Form Mutuals.

Besides the on-premise bolita ball drawings, operators employed various methods for determining winning numbers. On a national scale, selecting numbers included tabulating the pari-mutuel bets from a predetermined racetrack (left), using the last three digits of the US Treasury balance, or checking the total business on the New York Stock Exchange printed daily in the newspaper. In the early 1960s, with Miami's Cuban refugee population on the rise, bolita operators began using the last three digits of the Cuban National Lottery, whose numbers were broadcast over the radio every Saturday afternoon (below). By 1967, the Internal Revenue Service estimated that 20 million Americans had indulged in this gambling pastime, which generated a whopping $5 billion a year for the mob. Although seemingly harmless, these enormous profits contributed to much more sinister activities, including loan-sharking, narcotics, prostitution, and murder. (Both, author's collection.)

VALOR NOMINAL 22¢
PRECIO AL PUBLICO 25¢
REPUBLICA DE CUBA
INSTITUTO NACIONAL DE AHORRO Y VIVIENDAS

45ᴬ

28790
DOS OCHO SIETE NUEVE CERO

CUARENTA
Y CINCO

ESTATUA DE MARTI · LA HABANA

CUARENTA
Y CINCO

SORTEO Nº 48
FEBRERO 27, 1960

These suspects were brought to police headquarters for questioning after a 1965 raid on a bolita gambling operation. During the 1960s, bolita raids in South Florida were common, and law enforcement rounded up both operators and participants alike. From left to right are Ralph Alfanso, Guido Rodriguez, and John Rose, with the latter two using whatever available material to conceal their appearance from the photographer's camera. (Author's collection.)

Disguised detectives analyze receipts found at a bolita gambling house following a raid. To avoid exposure, bolita operators would constantly relocate the bank and habitually destroy records as to not leave an implicating paper trail. Often, collectors wrote bets on magician's flash paper, a type of paper chemically treated to turn to ash at the touch of a lighted cigarette. (Author's collection.)

Among the local bolita kingpins operating without national organized crime affiliations were Howard Pinder (foreground) and his son Howard Pinder Jr. (background), seen here exiting their bolita house following a November 1958 raid conducted by special agents of the IRS. When interrogated, both father and son refused to estimate the gross amount of wagers accepted, claiming the operation was only in business for a one-month period before the raid. (HistoryMiami Museum, 1989-011-22939.)

Upon searching the premises, agents found large sums of cash, betting slips, adding machine tape, and a collection sheet with various code names and balances (right), all typical paraphernalia employed in the operation of bolita. Protecting his son, Pinder Sr. claimed to be the sole operator of the lottery, asserting that Pinder Jr. worked merely as an unpaid bookkeeper—a claim that was later dismissed when the pair stood trial to determine their tax assessment. (HistoryMiami Museum, 1989-011-22944.)

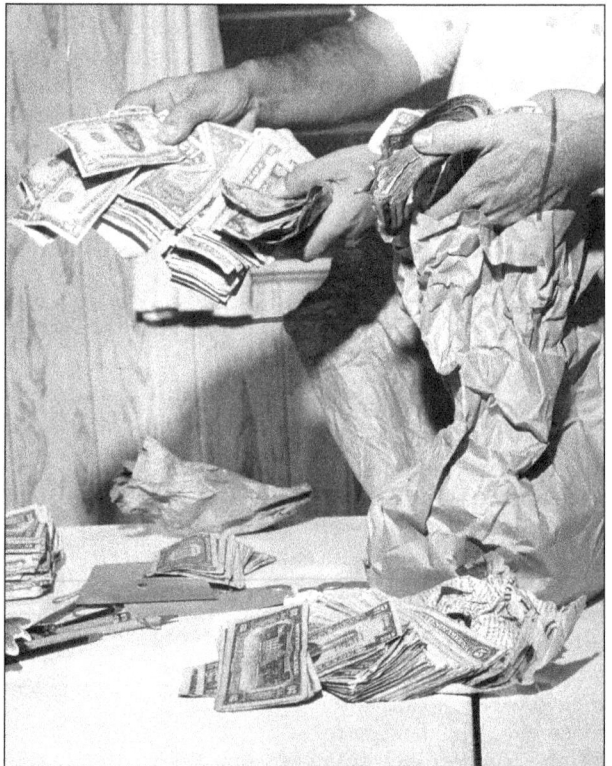

Hyman "Pittsburgh Hymie" Martin started his criminal career as a Pittsburgh mobster and bootlegger. In 1931, Martin was convicted of killing Cleveland city councilman William E. Potter, who organized crime figures believed was about to reveal information regarding crooked deals. Martin won a retrial and was later acquitted of the murder charge. Once a free man, Martin moved to South Florida and became a racket boss in the bolita lottery. (Author's collection.)

In 1965, Miami-Dade County investigators identified 35 "bolita houses," headquarters where operators added up all their gambling action. From the 35 houses identified, Hymie Martin was believed to be the banker of at least 14, with an estimated weekly gross of $300,000. Below is a detective's chart detailing Martin's South Florida bolita operations, along with his main associates and their respective territories. (Author's collection.)

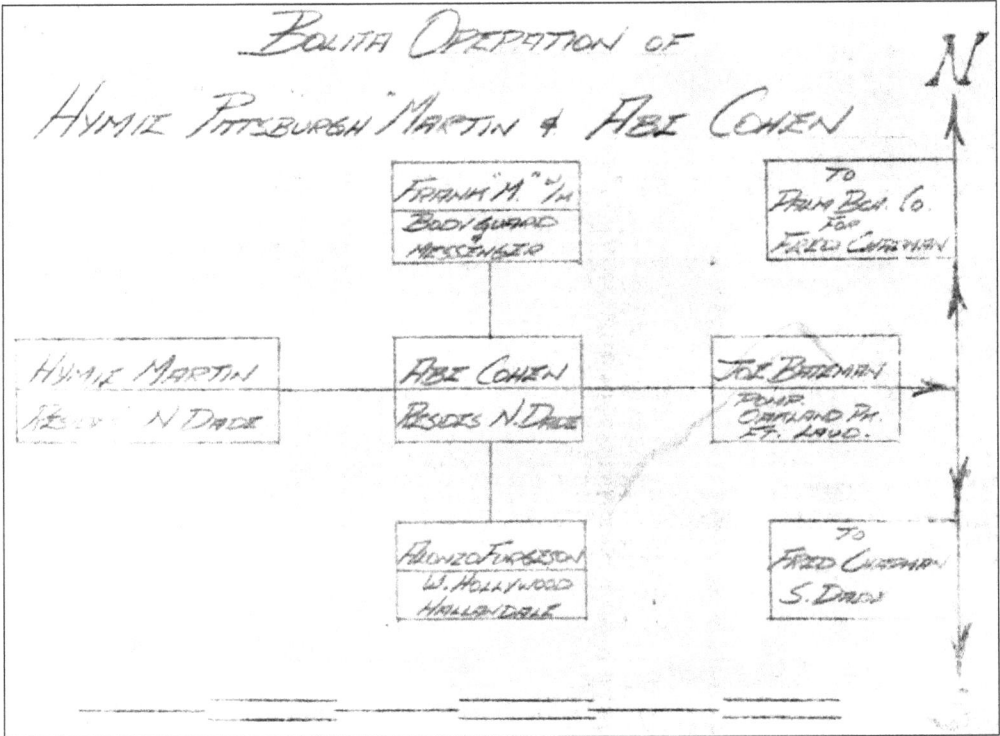

High-end bettors preferred Martin's operation, as he accepted a $20 parlay, while other local operators refused anything over $3. With the acceptance of such large bets, payouts could total $40,000 on a winning parlay, which could be multiplied if an individual wagered with several of Martin's lieutenants. Pictured above is the Broward County Burger Farm, an investment property owned by Martin and possibly used for his bolita operations. (Author's collection.)

By 1966, Martin had been sentenced to a six-month jail term for contempt of court after refusing to testify before a grand jury investigating bolita. Martin, who was now appropriately named "Fat Hymie" for the fuller shape he had acquired since his triggerman days in Pittsburgh, is seen here sitting smugly in the office of Judge Balaban. (Author's collection.)

Tampa mob boss Santo Trafficante Jr. poses for his mug shot after an arrest on November 16, 1953. He was picked up for general investigation and released. Trafficante was recognized as the most powerful organized crime figure in Florida, with the exception of the southeast coast, which was regarded as an open territory. Throughout the second half of the 1950s, Trafficante spent the majority of his time in Cuba overseeing operations for a number of casinos in which he reputedly held an interest, including the Deauville, Capri, Havana Hilton, and his main casino, the Sans Souci. Following the Cuban Revolution in 1959, Trafficante was forced to leave Cuba, and rather than return to Tampa where he would receive unwanted attention as the sole mafia kingpin, Trafficante decided to relocate to Miami. There, he could blend in with his gangster contemporaries from New York and Chicago while expanding his local bolita operations. Realizing that anti-Castro Cuban exiles would flock to Miami to start a new life, Trafficante positioned himself as a familiar, friendly face offering gambling and other illegal services to homesick Cubans. (Author's collection.)

Besides his gambling interest, Trafficante was heavily involved in the narcotics trade. In 1962, Trafficante sent Frank Furci, son of his top lieutenant Dominick Furci, to Vietnam to establish new distribution lines for heroin trafficking into the United States. Furci, as seen here in his 1962 travel visa to Vietnam, proved successful in his ventures, and in 1968, Trafficante himself traveled to the Far East to meet with his young emissary. (Author's collection.)

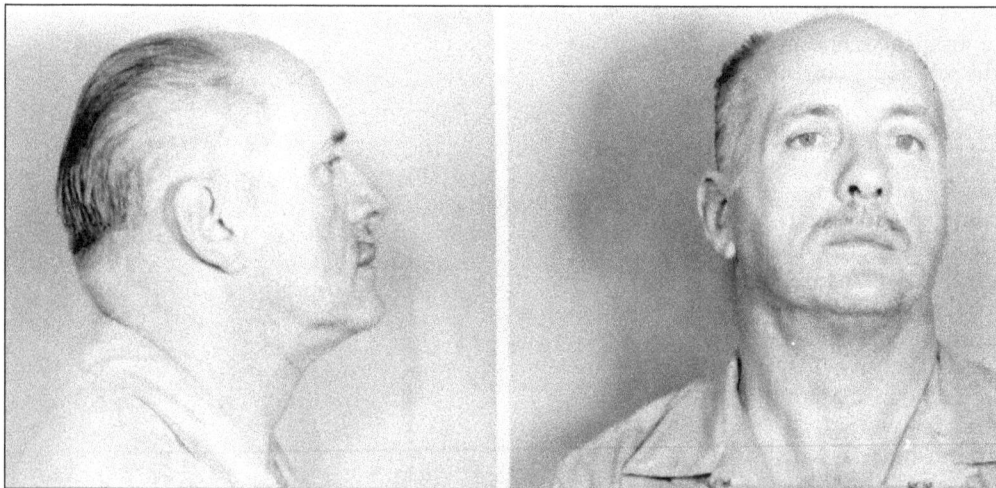

Evaristo Garcia Vidal, who ran a Miami bolita operation on behalf of the Trafficante organization, was arrested on May 27, 1967, and charged with violation of the Federal Wagering Tax Stamp Law. According to FBI documents, a Miami deputy sheriff admitted the reason for Vidal's arrest was that he refused to pay a $100 weekly protection fee, which Vidal believed he was exempt from due to his close relationship with Trafficante. (Author's collection.)

96

Jose Miguel Battle was the founder of The Corporation, a criminal organization consisting of Cuban American mobsters involved in bolita, loan-sharking, drug trafficking, and murder. As a former Cuban police officer serving under Fulgencio Batista, Battle learned the ins and outs of the gambling business while watching American mobsters make millions before the 1959 Cuban Revolution. (HistoryMiami Museum, 1995-277-10253.)

Following Castro's takeover, Jose Miguel Battle fled to Miami, where he was recruited by the CIA to train Cuban exiles volunteering as soldiers for the Bay of Pigs Invasion. Battle, who also volunteered, was captured along with 1,200 other soldiers and held as a prisoner of war for nearly two years. Following an agreement to exchange the surviving prisoners for $53 million in food and medicine, Pres. John F. Kennedy and his wife, Jacqueline, attended a veterans' "welcome back" ceremony at Miami's Orange Bowl Stadium. (Author's collection.)

Upon his return from Cuba, Jose Miguel Battle, nicknamed "El Padrino" (Spanish for "The Godfather"), settled in New Jersey and immediately fell into a life of crime, muscling in on various vices, including strip clubs, cockfighting, and the most lucrative, bolita. During the 1970s, Battle's crime ring, known as La Corporacion, was generating an estimated $45 million annually from their activities in Latin America, New York, and Florida. In 1977, Battle was convicted in connection with the death of Ernesto Torres, a top hit man for The Corporation who was murdered in Opa-Locka following a fallout with Battle. However, an appeals court overturned his 30-year jail sentence, and Battle pled guilty to murder conspiracy in exchange for a sentence of two years' time served. Battle continued to expand his gambling operations and, by 1987, was listed as one of Dade County's wealthiest residents, with a net worth of $175 million. Above, Battle poses with his pet monkey at his $1.5 million, 30-acre Miami ranch in June 1985. (HistoryMiami Museum, 1995-277-10252.)

Seven

GANG WARS AND MOB HITS

Among the most appealing aspects of South Florida for organized crime figures was the shared understanding of an open city, free of territorial wars that were common back home. Besides occasional breaches, the treaty was strongly respected for the first half of the 20th century, until a new class of criminals, displaying a complete disregard for their founders' guidelines, arrived in the 1960s and waged gang warfare that resulted in murders, bombings, and a general negligence for public safety. With the intentions of calming a fearful public, Claude Kirk (right), Florida's 36th governor, conducted a "war on crime" and vowed to drive organized criminals from Florida. (Author's collection.)

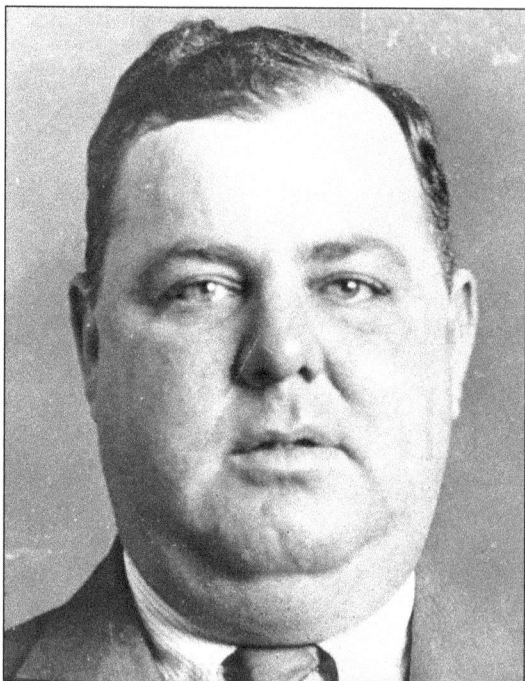

Thomas "Fatty" Walsh (left) was a former gunman and bodyguard for New York gambler Arnold Rothstein and reputed successor to Rothstein's narcotics ring following his November 1928 murder. In January 1929, Walsh moved to Miami but soon suffered a similar fate to his former boss when, just three months later, he was shot and killed while sitting at a card table at the Biltmore Hotel, branding Walsh with the unique distinction of being Miami's first high-profile gangland murder. Walsh's associate Arthur L. Clark (bottom right), who followed Walsh to Miami where they shared a house in Coral Gables, was also shot and wounded by the lone gunman. Aside from a small interest in the Biltmore's gambling room, New York authorities claimed that Walsh was in Miami to sell a large quantity of stolen jewelry to wealthy hotel guests vacationing in Miami. (Both, author's collection.)

Investigators who believed the Miami slaying of Walsh was connected to the New York murder of Arnold Rothstein searched for clues that would link the two homicides and provide insight into the Rothstein murder that was garnering national attention. After questioning more than a dozen witnesses and associates, the state attorney issued a first-degree warrant for Eddie Wilson, a New York and Chicago gambler who operated the gaming room at the Biltmore Hotel (above) and disappeared immediately after the shooting. It was later determined that the two homicides were not related, and Wilson shot Walsh over disputes in their shared gambling enterprise. Below, Assistant State Attorney Richard Hunt (left) and Sheriff M.P. Lehman (right) examine bullet and fingerprint marks on the card table where Walsh was shot and killed. (Both, author's collection.)

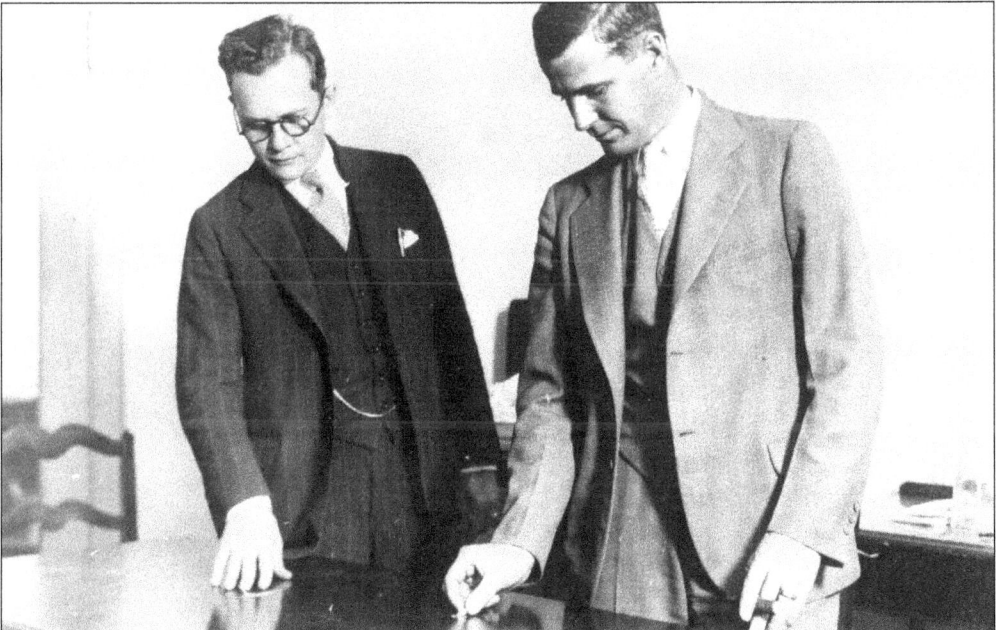

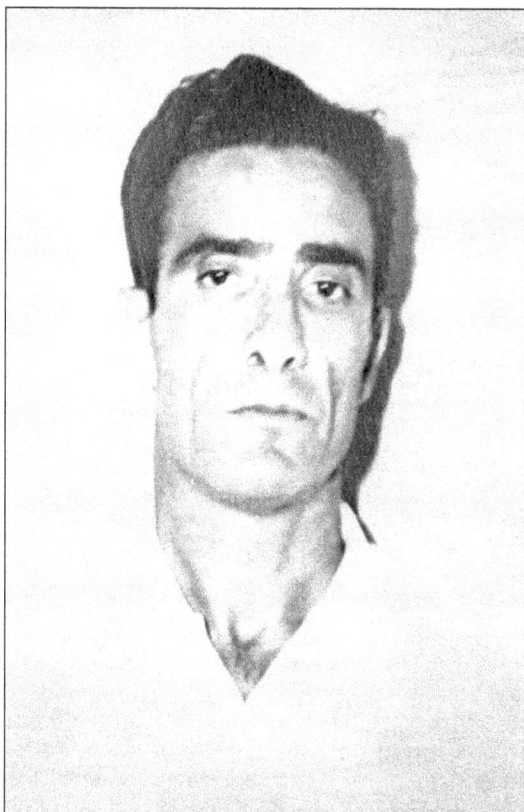

Thomas "The Enforcer" Altamura was a made member of the Gambino family and a top loan shark operating out of Miami's ritzy North Bay Village neighborhood. Always sharply attired, Tommy A., as he was known by friends and associates, would often hobnob with celebrities and millionaires while frequenting Miami's hottest clubs and lounges. In addition to loan-sharking, Altamura had connections with gambling, labor racketeering, narcotics, and contract murder, including the 1958 slaying of Tampa independent bolita operator Joe Pelusa Diaz, ordered by Santo Trafficante Jr. Altamura was identified as the shooter but avoided conviction when prosecutors determined the witness's partial identification was not sufficient. In 1967, Altamura entered a feud with local hoodlum Tony Esperti that concluded in his death on Halloween morning, just steps through the front door of the Harbor Lounge (below). (Left, author's collection; below, HistoryMiami Museum, 1989-011-6782.)

Anthony "Big Tony" Esperti was a well-known Miami hoodlum with arrests and charges for burglary, assault, extortion, and eventually murder. In his earlier years, Esperti was a professional heavyweight boxer who started his pugilistic career in Queens, New York. Never a major contender in the ring, Esperti moved to Miami after a 10-month prison stint for unlawful entry and began hanging out at the world-famous 5th Street Gym. While training at the gym, Esperti was approached by legendary boxing promoter Chris Dundee and asked to fight recent Olympic gold medalist Cassius Clay. Although out of shape, Esperti was strapped for cash and agreed to fight the up-and-coming boxer in a bout that took place at the Miami Beach Auditorium on January 17, 1961. After just three rounds, Clay won the fight by a TKO when the referee stopped the fight. (Both, author's collection.)

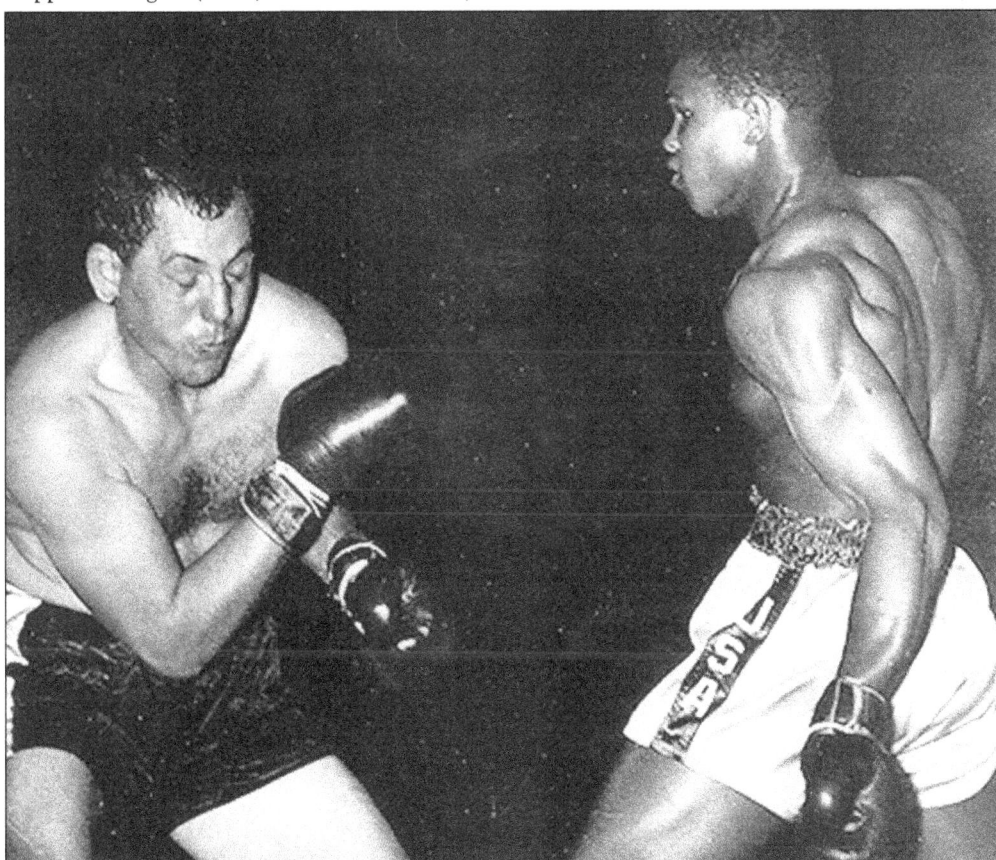

Above is an aerial photograph of The Place for Steak restaurant on the 79th Street Causeway, along with the attached after-hours watering hole, the Harbor Lounge. It was here in the opening hours of Halloween morning that mafia lieutenant Thomas Altamura was gunned down by local thug and strongman Tony Esperti. Below is the marble-floored, brick-enclosed foyer of the Harbor Lounge where Thomas Altamura took his final steps. Within seconds of spotting Altamura's entrance through the doorway, Esperti stood from the bar, approached Tommy A. with his gun drawn, and shot five bullets into the gangster's head and body. (Both, Miami-Dade Municipal Archives.)

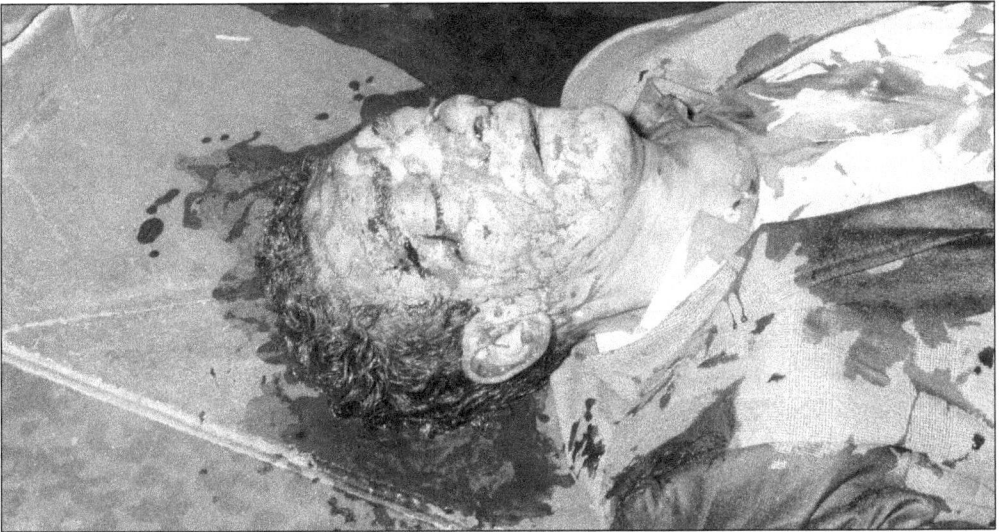

The lifeless body of Thomas Altamura lies in a pool of blood at the entrance of the Harbour Lounge. Using a .38-caliber revolver, Tony Esperti ended the dapper gangster's life with two bullets into Altamura's head, followed by three more shots into his body. The feud between Altamura and Esperti allegedly stemmed from a turf war between the two men, who were both looking to expand their extortion and loan-sharking operations in Miami. One month before the Altamura slaying, Esperti survived a bomb blast at Happy Storks Lounge, another late-night hot spot on the 79th Street Causeway. Then a week before the murder, Esperti attacked one of Altamura's men who had previously been in an altercation with a friend of his. Altamura vowed to settle the score personally; however, Esperti, witnessing Altamura's entrance into the lounge, preemptively beat him to the shot. (Both, Miami-Dade Municipal Archives.)

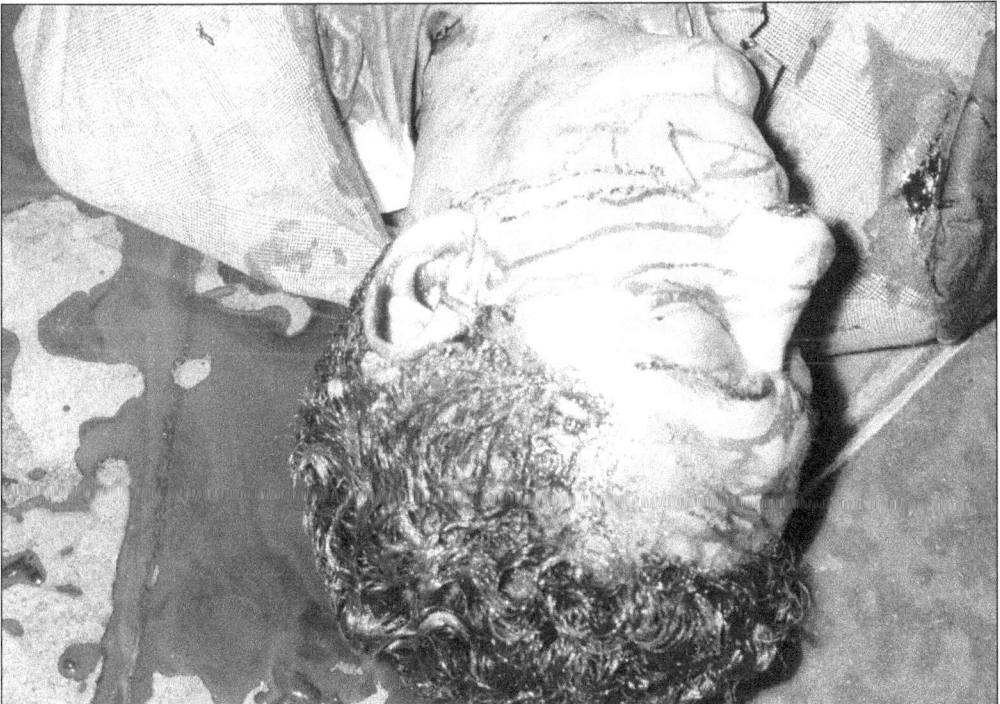

Frank "Lefty" Rosenthal (center) was a professional sports handicapper, Las Vegas casino executive, and longtime associate of organized crime figures. Often considered the greatest handicapper in the country, Rosenthal started his betting career in Chicago but, after an indictment in the early 1960s, moved his operation to North Bay Village in Miami to avoid future harassment from the Chicago authorities. While living in Miami, Rosenthal earned a national reputation as one of the top sports handicappers in the country, setting odds for professional basketball, football, baseball, and hockey, as well as college basketball and football. Throughout the 1960s, Rosenthal faced a series of arrests in Miami for illegal gambling and bookmaking and was a leading suspect in the bombing of multiple businesses and cars, which forced him to relocate once again, this time setting his sights on the gamblers' paradise of Las Vegas. Above, Rosenthal is pictured with his longtime Vegas associate, Chicago mobster Anthony "The Ant" Spliotro, and Spilotro's wife, Nancy. (Author's collection.)

Samuel Solomon Green (left) and Frank "Lefty" Rosenthal (center) are pictured after their November 1965 arrest at the Multiple Sports News Service on charges of illegal interstate transmission of betting information. Rosenthal served as a consultant for the Miami-based sports service and set the line or spread for a game. In 1963, Rosenthal was convicted of bribing an NYU basketball player for shaving points in a college basketball game. (Author's collection.)

Samuel Solomon Green, president of the Multiple Sports News Service on 79th Street in North Bay Village, was arrested on May 25, 1966, along with 16 other men, during a nationwide crackdown on interstate telephone transmission of gambling information. Using an electronic device called a blue box, Green shared information cross-country by phone while avoiding long-distance billing and call records, usually a telltale sign for law enforcement monitoring gambling. (Author's collection.)

Within the first six months of 1967, Miami was rocked by half a dozen gang-related bombings, with targets including homes, stores, and automobiles. According to the testimony of Ricardo "The Monkey" Morales Navarette, a Cuban exile allegedly trained as a CIA operative, Frank "Lefty" Rosenthal hired Navarette to perform a string of bombings across Miami. On June 3, an unoccupied car belonging to the wife of bookie Mickey Zion was bombed in North Bay Village (above). Two weeks later, on June 16, Rosenthal hired Navarette to bomb Aflie's Newsstand on Alton Road—a job that was previously botched the month before when the neighboring Epicure Market was mistakenly bombed. The newsstand's bombing was ordered after its owner Alfie Mart, a successful bookie, refused to use the gambling sheets issued by Rosenthal's Multiple Sports News Service. Rosenthal paid Navarette $1,000 for each bombing and specifically instructed that no one be injured, as the bombings were solely ordered to send a message. (Author's collection.)

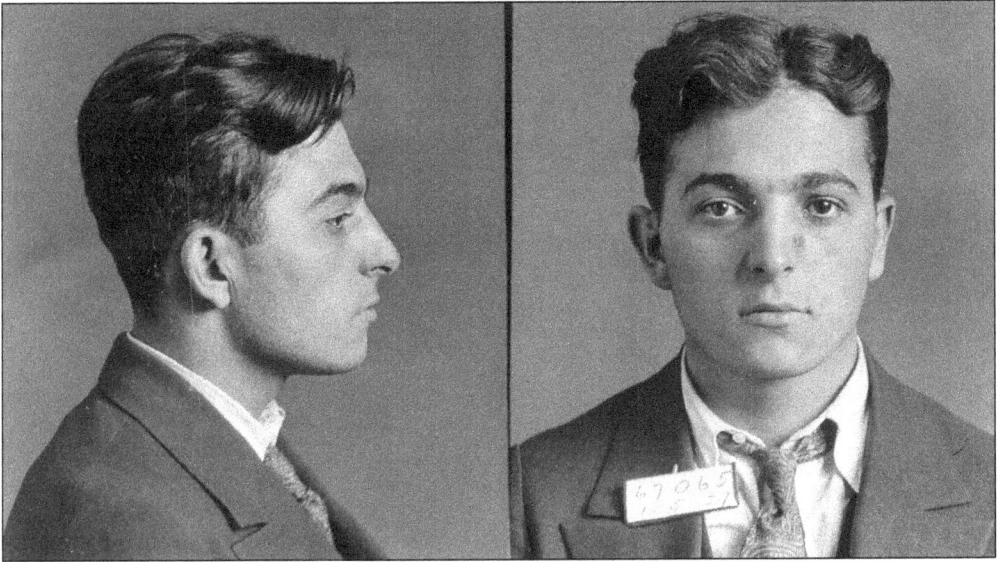

John "Futto" Biello, seen above in a 1927 NYPD mug shot, was a capo in the Genovese crime family. Biello unexpectedly hit it big in October 1961 when his nightclub, the Peppermint Lounge, suddenly became the hottest club in town and the epicenter of America's latest dance craze, the Twist. With his sudden success, Biello was ready to maneuver away from a life of crime and, two months later, moved to Miami to open a sister location on the 79th Street Causeway. The club was an immediate success, and patrons watched as celebrities, socialites, and mobsters mingled among the candy-cane, red-and-white-striped walls. Notable guests included Dion, Conway Twitty, comedian Lenny Bruce, and the Beatles, pictured below with the B.G. Ramblers at Miami's Peppermint Lounge just four days after their first performance on *The Ed Sullivan Show*. (Above, author's collection; below, HistoryMiami Museum, 1989-011-6100.)

With the success of Miami's Peppermint Lounge in full swing, Biello continued his transition from New York gangster to respectable Miami club owner, living quietly in his Miami Shores home. However, Biello's past caught up with him, and in 1964, mob boss Joseph Bonanno, looking to consolidate the New York crime families, approached Biello and asked for assistance in eliminating rival mob boss Tommy Lucchese (above) during one of his frequent visits to South Florida. Instead, Biello exposed the assassination plot, and Bonanno was mercifully forced to retire to his Arizona home. On March 17, 1967, Biello was shot six times while entering the passenger seat of his car in a Miami Beach parking lot (below). The murder, believed to have been ordered by Bonanno for Biello's betrayal, was purportedly carried out by mob hit man George Barone. (Above, author's collection; below, *Miami Herald*.)

Following his participation in the unsuccessful plot to assassinate Cuban communist leader Fidel Castro, John "Handsome Johnny" Roselli, seen here in an early LAPD mug shot, returned to the West Coast and continued his involvement in gambling throughout Las Vegas and Los Angeles. (Los Angeles Police Department.)

In June 1975, Roselli was called to testify before the US Senate Select Committee on Intelligence about his relationship with the CIA and the plan to kill Castro. A week before his testimony, Sam Giancana, Roselli's partner in the operation, was shot and killed in his Illinois home, prompting Roselli to retire his operations and leave the West Coast for Miami. Roselli is seen here entering the Senate investigation. (Author's collection.)

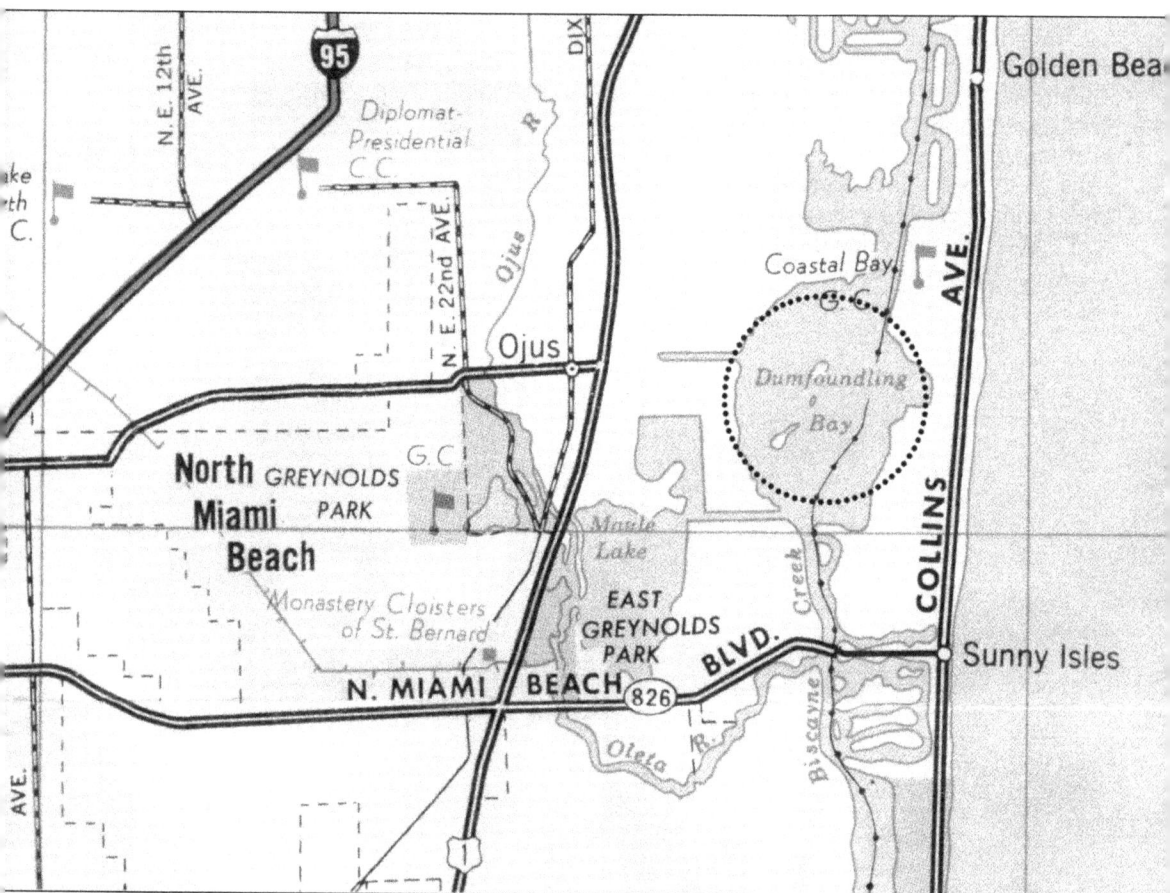

One year after his initial testimony, the US Senate Select Committee recalled Rosselli for further testimony regarding his knowledge of the Kennedy assassination; however, he had gone missing at about the same time. On August 9, 1976, local fishermen reported a 55-gallon steel oil drum floating in North Miami Beach's Dumfoundling Bay (circled above). Once opened, authorities discovered Roselli's decomposing body stuffed inside the chain-wrapped drum. After examination, it was ruled Roselli had died of asphyxiation before being dismembered, interred in the drum, and dumped in the bay—an exact location could not be determined because of the bay's currents. The Senate Select Committee launched an investigation into Roselli's murder, seeking a link with the CIA's plot to kill Castro and a supposed Cuban counterplot against President Kennedy, of which Roselli informed the committee. After initial hesitation, the FBI entered the Roselli murder case. However, unable to turn up any solid evidence linking his death to his Senate testimony, the investigation eventually ruled the murder a typical gangland slaying. (Author's collection.)

John B. Callahan was a prominent Boston businessman and a mobster associate who fraternized with Boston's biggest gangsters, including notorious Winter Hill Gang leaders James "Whitey" Bulger, Steve "Rifleman" Flemmi, and John "The Executioner" Martorano. Callahan admitted to meeting individuals with questionable reputations but categorically denied any business involvement with reputed organized crime members. (US government.)

In 1974, Callahan was named the president of World Jai-Alai Association, whose main office was based in Miami (above) but had betting operations with frontons throughout Connecticut and Florida. After only two years, Callahan stepped down from the presidency following an investigation into his mob connections, which threatened the company's chances of securing additional licensing. In 1981, World Jai-Alai owner Roger Wheeler suspected Callahan was involved in a $10,000 weekly skimming operation from the Jai-Alai's cash concessions. Wheeler launched an investigation into his company's finances but was murdered on May 27, 1981, while entering his Cadillac after a game of golf at a country club in Tulsa, Oklahoma. (Author's collection.)

After the murder of World Jai-Alai owner Roger Wheeler, Brian Halloran, a cocaine dealer and associate of the Winter Hill Gang, approached the FBI and offered information connecting Bulger and Flemmi to the murder in exchange for witness protection. Tipped off by their FBI contact John Connolly, Flemmi later testified that Bulger gunned down Halloran while he was exiting a South Side Boston bar. Worried that Callahan would fold under interrogation regarding the murders connected to World Jai-Ali, Bulger and Flemmi agreed Callahan was too big a liability and had to go. On August 2, 1982, Callahan's decomposing body was discovered in the backseat of his Cadillac parked at Miami International Airport (above). James Bulger, seen below in an early Miami Beach mug shot, spent parts of his teenage years living in a rooming house on North Miami Avenue and painting cars at Johnnie & Mack's auto body shop. (Above, US Government; below, Miami Beach Police Department.)

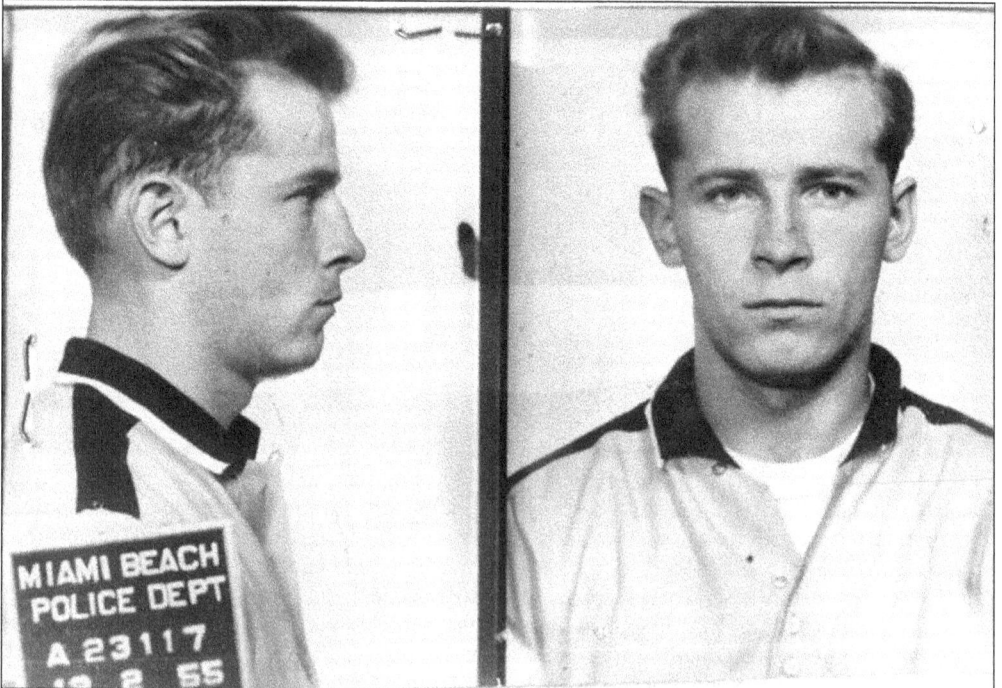

Eight

Lansky's Legend

Following the Kefauver Committee's exposure in 1950, Meyer Lansky was forced to relocate the majority of his gambling interest to Cuba and Las Vegas but remained a prominent force in South Florida. Regardless of where his business interests lay, Lansky always maintained his Miami presence, and by the time of his death in 1983, it seemed almost every Miami local had a story of the time they encountered Lansky. Above, Lansky takes his shih tzu, Bruzzer, for a walk on Miami Beach. (Author's collection.)

Morris Lansburgh first came to Miami Beach from Baltimore in 1940 after liquidating his holdings in his father's small distillery company and moving south to join his father in a hotel venture. Along with business partner Sam Cohen (not of the S&G Syndicate), Lansburgh eventually became one of the top hoteliers in the area, operating eight of the largest hotels on Miami Beach's "Hotel Row." At one point, Lansburgh's credentials included membership in the Miami Beach Tourist Development Authority, head of the Miami Beach Hotel Association, and president of Associated Resort Hotels. In 1960, Lansburgh entered a public business transaction with Meyer Lansky that ultimately led the hotelier and his partner to jail time and a tarnished reputation in Miami Beach. (Author's collection.)

116

This 1960s aerial photograph of Miami Beach's Gold Coast depicts the holdings of the Lansburgh and Cohen combine at the height of their power. Meyer Lansky reputedly held an interest in the group of highly profitable hotels, though successfully hid his shares through a labyrinth of corporations, deeds, mortgages, leases, and subleases—a common, intricate process devised to extract untraceable cash. The group's eight hotels included the Deauville, Sans Souci, Saxony, Casablanca, Sherry Frontenac, Versailles, Crown, and Eden Roc. Under the collective roofs of all eight hotels housed a steady population of roughly 6,000 guests. In addition to their Miami Beach hotels, their firm also owned hotels in the Bahamas and Spain. (Author's collection.)

Morris Lansburgh (center), pictured with friends and the Orange Bowl beauty queen candidates, enjoys an evening out at the Sans Souci Hotel in 1957. With the tremendous success of their Miami Beach hotels, Lansburgh and Cohen desired to expand their operations and establish their presence in the booming city of Las Vegas. In May 1960, Meyer Lansky provided the opportunity when he brokered the $10.6 million sale between the Miami Beach hotel magnates and Albert

Parvin, owner of the Las Vegas Flamingo, a hotel-casino in which Lansky had held an interest since its inception in December 1946. For his efforts, Lansky collected a $200,000 finder's fee, which because of the legality of the transaction, he claimed as an annual salary, divided into 32 quarterly installments of $6,250 over an eight-year period. (Author's collection.)

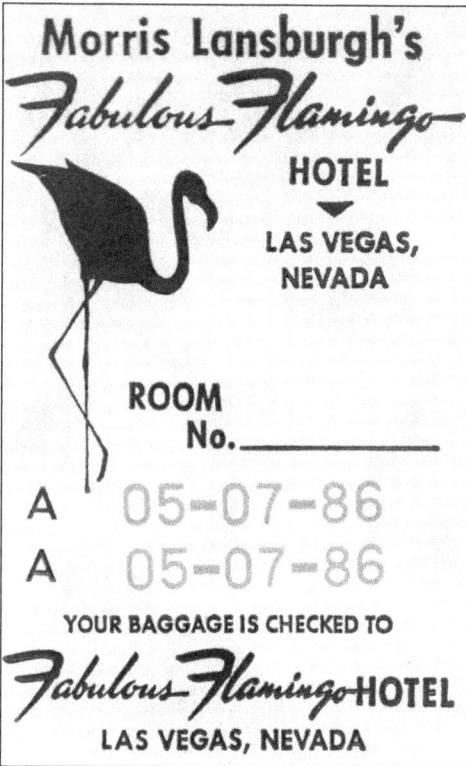

Morris Lansburgh's
Fabulous Flamingo
HOTEL
▼
LAS VEGAS,
NEVADA

ROOM
No._____

A   05-07-86

A   05-07-86

YOUR BAGGAGE IS CHECKED TO

Fabulous Flamingo HOTEL
LAS VEGAS, NEVADA

Lansburgh's corporation successfully operated the Flamingo Hotel from 1960 until its sale in 1967. However, in 1971, Morris Lansburgh, Sam Cohen, Meyer Lansky, and two others were charged with skimming more than $14 million during the group's seven-year control of the hotel. The skim operation, attributed to Lansky, was the removal and distribution of untaxed revenue. Pictured here is a Flamingo baggage tag bearing Lansburgh's name during his period of ownership. (Author's collection.)

In January 1973, three weeks before their trial, Lansburgh and Cohen pled guilty to conspiracy of hiding casino revenues and evading taxes. Both men were sentenced to one year in prison and a $20,000 fine, while Lansky, recuperating from open-heart surgery, had his trial postponed. At right, Lansburgh talks with Jackie Gleason after gifting him an Eden Roc bathrobe during a 1968 testimonial dinner in Gleason's honor. (Author's collection.)

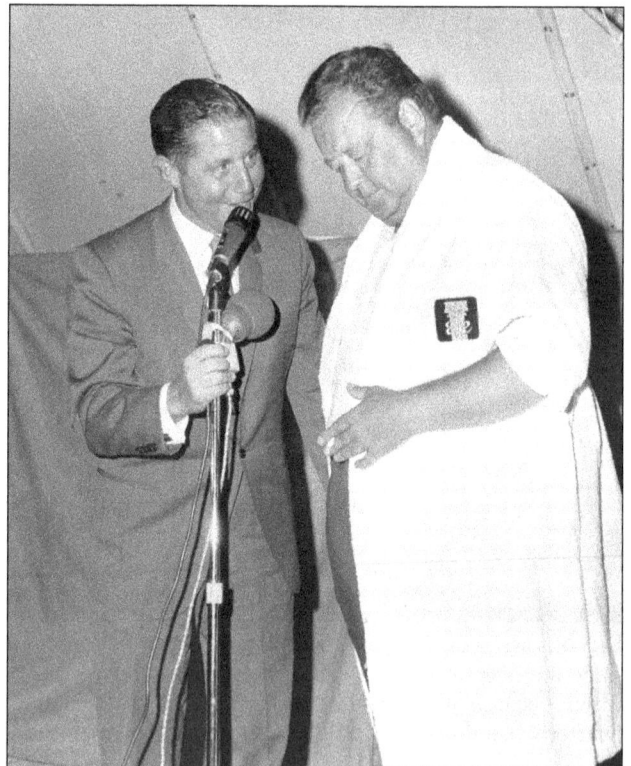

In addition to the luxurious Miami Beach hotels, Meyer Lansky was believed to secretly control a group of 19 one- to two-story beachfront motels located on the famed "Motel Row" in Sunny Isles, just 10 miles north of Miami Beach. The motels were openly operated by a group known as the Minneapolis Combination, which consisted of Isadore "Kid Cann" Blumenfeld (above) and his brothers Harry and Yiddy Bloom. Cann was considered the biggest mobster in Minnesota's history, making a name for himself during Prohibition when his gang oversaw bootlegging, prostitution, and labor racketeering throughout Minneapolis. Maintaining a close friendship with Lansky dating back to the 1930s, Cann moved to Miami Beach in 1964 following a three-year prison sentence for white slavery and bribing a juror. Upon his arrival, Cann immediately began buying up South Florida real estate while he and his brothers also dabbled in illegal stock market trades and money laundering. (Author's collection.)

By 1969, the Minneapolis Combination was believed to control $40 million worth of real estate along Motel Row (above), including notable establishments such as the Sahara, Golden Nugget, Desert Inn, Aztec, and the Hawaiian Isle. On top of their motel leases, the Combination also owned the land on which the Fontainebleau was built, a half interest in the Eden Roc's land, and the Singapore Hotel (below), which they acquired via a trade for the Seacoast Towers South. On an almost daily basis, after walking his dog and breakfast at Wolfie's Deli, Meyer Lansky occupied the Singapore's second-floor card room as a base of operation. According to a Lansky associate, cash from the Vegas skim was brought by train to Miami, where Lansky and his partners met in the card room and distributed it among themselves by shares. (Author's collection.)

In December 1965, investigative journalist Hank Messick, working on a special assignment for the *Miami Herald*, wrote a three-part series claiming Lansky was not only the "biggest man in organized crime" but also had a net worth valued at $300 million. Following the *Herald* series, Lansky was now the most public organized crime figure in the county, dealing with constant FBI surveillance, wiretapping, and continuous newspaper articles publishing his photograph, associates, and criminal history. In March 1970, after a return flight from Mexico, Lansky was searched by airport customs agents, who discovered Donnatal, a sedative used for stomach ulcers, which required a prescription Lansky was unable to produce. Meyer was arrested and booked in a Dade County jail, and although his lawyer easily had the drug charges dismissed, the latest harassment was the final straw. Fed up with America and the possibility of impending convictions, Lansky traveled to Tel Aviv in hopes of gaining Israeli citizenship and a permanent new residence. Above, Meyer Lansky looks optimistically toward the future in his 1970 passport photograph. (Author's collection.)

With a 12-week travel visa, Meyer Lansky, his wife Teddy, and their dog Bruzzer arrived in Israel in the summer of 1970. Their main objective was to seek asylum under Israel's Law of Return, a legislation passed in 1950 that allowed Jews from around the world to live and gain citizenship in Israel. However, a 1954 provision excluded Jews with a criminal past. When Lansky applied for citizenship, his reputation had already reached Israeli media, leading Prime Minister Golda Meir and Interior Minister Yosef Burg to emphatically deny his request. Above, after two years in Israel, a defeated Meyer Lansky, escorted by two FBI agents, walks through Miami International Airport following his return home on November 7, 1972. When his wife Teddy arrived three days later, an altercation ensued when a television reporter called her "Godmother," for which Teddy spat in her face. (Both, author's collection.)

Once back home, Meyer Lansky prepared to face the three indictments brought against him while abroad in Israel: contempt of court, casino skimming, and tax evasion. Lansky's lawyer, E. David Rosen (above left), lost the contempt charge but was victorious in discrediting Vincent "Fat Vinnie" Teresa (below), the government informant who testified against Lansky in the tax evasion case. Rosen's biggest obstacle was the casino skimming charge, which, if convicted, would result in a prison sentence of up to eight years. Rosen successfully petitioned to have the case transferred to Nevada, but when Lansky was called to appear, doctors ruled the aging Lansky too sick to travel, and after multiple hearings, the indictment was dismissed. On November 3, 1976, Meyer Lansky, finally a free man, was allowed to peacefully live out the remainder of his life in Miami. (Both, author's collection.)

Above, in a photograph reminiscent of Hyman Roth's cake-cutting scene in the *The Godfather Part II*, Meyer Lansky (left) makes the ceremonial first cut of his 80th birthday cake, in the company of friends Bob Barraso (center) and Vincent "Jimmy Blue Eyes" Alo. In December 1974, Lansky phoned actor Lee Strasberg, who portrayed the Lansky-inspired Roth, to grant his approval and to congratulate Strasberg on his critically acclaimed performance, for which Lansky had just one criticism: "Now why couldn't you have made me more sympathetic?" Lansky half jokingly asked, "After all, I am a grandfather." Below, Meyer and friends pose for a photograph at his 80th birthday party, representing 50 years of friendship. From left to right are Jake Lansky, Vincent Alo, Meyer Lansky, and Harry "Nig Rosen" Stromberg. During the 1930s and 1940s, these four men controlled the majority of South Florida gambling from Hollywood to Miami Beach. (Both, author's collection.)

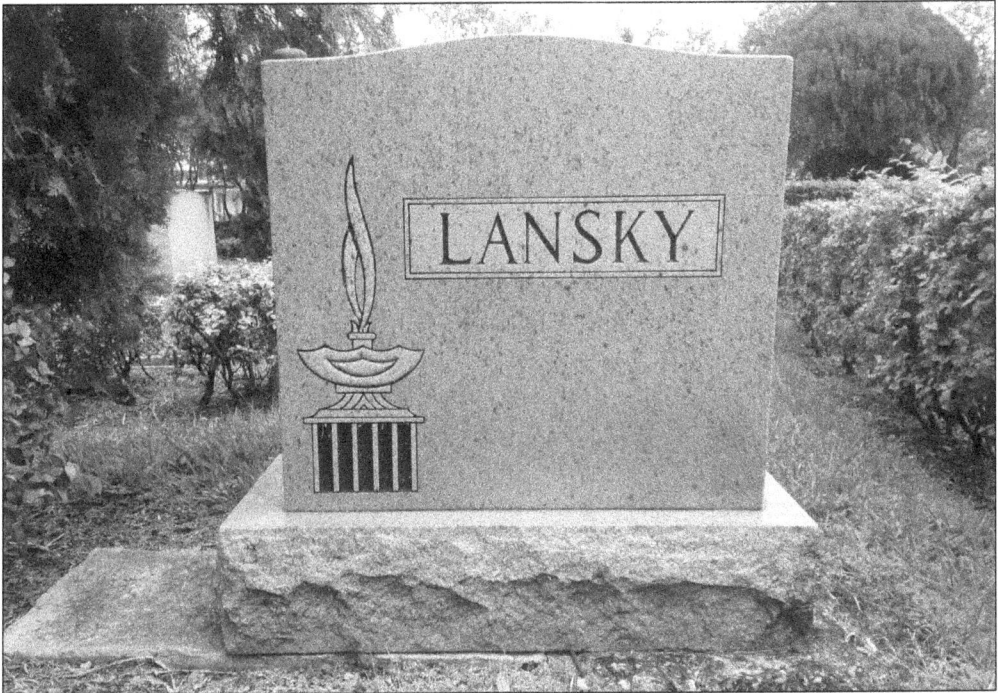

Throughout the 1970s, Lansky's health began to decline. A lifelong smoker, Lansky kicked the habit in 1973 to undergo heart surgery, but the three-pack-a-day habit eventually caught up with him, and by the late 1970s, Lansky had developed lung cancer. Optimistic doctors removed a portion of his lung, but over time, the cancer returned and spread throughout his body. Weak and frail, Lansky spent the last few years of his life living as comfortably as possible at the Imperial House in Miami Beach, often meeting with old friends and associates to reminisce about the past. On January 15, 1983, surrounded by family at Mount Sinai Hospital, Lansky fell asleep, never to awake again. His body was buried at the Mount Nebo Cemetery in South Miami, where his eldest son, Buddy, would be buried beside him six years later. (Both photographs by Avi Bash.)

Visit us at
arcadiapublishing.com

www.ingramcontent.com/pod-product-compliance
Lightning Source LLC
Chambersburg PA
CBHW050712110426
42813CB00007B/2158